COMING TO TERMS WITH SIN

A Study of Romans 1-5

BIBLE STUDY GUIDE

From the Bible-teaching ministry of

Charles R. Swindoll

INSIGHT FOR LIVING

Chuck graduated in 1963 from Dallas Theological Seminary, where he now serves as the school's fourth president, helping to prepare a new generation of men and women for the ministry. Chuck has served in pastorates in three states: Massachusetts, Texas, and California, including almost twenty-three years at the First Evangelical Free Church in Fullerton, California. His sermon messages have been aired over radio since 1979 as the *Insight for Living* broadcast. A best-selling author, Chuck has written numerous books and booklets on many subjects.

Based on the outlines and transcripts of Chuck's sermons, the study guide text is co-authored by Gary Matlack, a graduate of Texas Tech University and Dallas Theological Seminary. He also wrote the Living Insights sections.

Editor in Chief:
Cynthia Swindoll
Director, Educational Ministries:
Gary Matlack
Senior Editor and Assistant Writer:
Wendy Peterson
Copy Editors:
Marco Salazar
Glenda Schlahta

Text Designer:
Gary Lett
Graphic System Administrator:
Bob Haskins
Publishing System Specialist:
Alex Pasieka
Director, Communications Division:
John Norton
Project Coordinator:
Shannon Scharkey

Unless otherwise identified, all Scripture references are from the New American Standard Bible, updated edition, copyright © The Lockman Foundation 1960, 1962, 1963, 1968, 1971, 1972, 1973, 1975, 1977, 1995. Used by permission. Scripture taken from the Holy Bible, New International Version © 1973, 1978, 1984 International Bible Society, used by permission of Zondervan Bible Publishers [NIV].

An effort has been made to locate sources and obtain permission where necessary for the quotations used in this book. In the event of any unintentional omission, a modification will gladly be incorporated in future printings.

ISBN 1-57972-257-1
Study Guide Cover Design: Eric Chimenti
Cover Art: Kevin N. Ghiglione/©The Stock Illustration Source
Printed in the United States of America

CONTENTS

INTRODUCTION

In all of Scripture, I know of no book more exacting, more serious, more demanding, or more life-changing than Paul's letter to the Romans. It is the apostle's magnum opus—a mind-stretching, heart-wrenching discourse on the righteousness of God granted in Christ and worked out in life.

When I preached this series as a pastor in California, I had every reason to believe that God would use this grand and glorious section of Scripture to change people. I still do.

A word of warning, though, as you begin this first volume, *Coming to Terms with Sin*. Gazing at Paul's picture of human sinfulness is anything but pleasant. But it's necessary. Only when we have come to terms with sin in all its fury are we able to come to Christ in all His glory.

Pray with me, won't you, that God would use these messages to help many understand and embrace that grace of God in Jesus Christ.

Chuck Swindoll

Chuck Swindoll

PUTTING TRUTH INTO ACTION

Knowledge apart from application falls short of God's desire for His children. He wants us to apply what we learn so that we will change and grow. This study guide was prepared with these goals in mind. As you go through the following pages, we hope your desire to discover biblical truth will grow as your understanding of God's Word increases and that you will be encouraged to apply what you've learned.

To assist you in your study, we've included a section called † **Living Insights** at the end of each lesson. These exercises will challenge you to study further and to think of specific ways to put your discoveries into action.

There are many ways to use this guide—in personal devotions, group studies, discussions with friends and family, and Sunday school classes. And, of course, it's an ideal study aid when you're listening to its corresponding *Insight for Living* radio series.

To benefit most from this study guide, we would encourage you to consider it a spiritual journal. That's why we've included space in the **Living Insights** for recording your thoughts and discoveries. We hope you'll return to those sections often for review and encouragement as you continue to grow in your walk with Christ.

Gary Matlack

Gary Matlack
Coauthor of Text
Author of Living Insights

COMING TO TERMS WITH SIN

A Study of Romans 1-5

KEY WORDS AND CONCEPTS IN ROMANS

We offer this list of theological terms to help you more fully understand and apply the rich truths found in Paul's letter to the Romans. We suggest you read through the list as you begin your study, then use it as a reference guide while working your way through Romans.

Condemnation: God's judicial pronouncement of sinful humanity's guilt before Him. It is a declaration of our depravity and the punishment we deserve for it. Condemnation is the opposite of justification, which is God's pronouncement of our righteousness in Christ. Once we place our trust in Christ, we are no longer under condemnation (Rom. 8:1). Rather, we are justified—pronounced righteous by God because we are clothed in the righteousness of His Son (Rom. 3:21–26; 5:1–2, 9).

Faith: The unqualified acceptance of and dependence on the completed work of Jesus Christ to secure God's mercy toward believers. It is the instrumental cause of our salvation, the means by which we are linked to Christ and allowed to receive God's gracious gift of justification. True faith includes *knowledge* that there is a holy God who gave His Son to reconcile sinners to Himself; *assent*, which means being intellectually convinced of the truth of that knowledge; and *volition*, being so convinced of the truth that we place our trust in Christ (Rom. 1:17; 3:22, 30; Heb. 11:1).

Flesh: Used in a theological sense, *flesh* doesn't refer to our physical body. Rather, it refers to our orientation and identity before God saved us—we were unbelievers, controlled and enslaved by sin, rejecters of God, people who preferred sin over righteousness. The flesh still tries to control us, but it no longer has any claim on us, since as Christians we now belong to Christ and walk in His Spirit (see Rom. 7:5, 14, 18, 25; 8:9).

Foreknowledge: In its most general sense, *foreknowledge* is God's knowing all things before they come to pass. It is more, though,

xiii

than God's simply having information ahead of time. God knows what will come to pass because He determines what will come to pass (see *predestination*). When specifically applied to salvation, foreknowledge is God's knowing us before we knew Him, before He even created us. When the Bible speaks of God's knowing people, it means He has made them the objects of His special love. Foreknowledge, then, is a word of determined choosing. God loved believers and chose them to be His own long before they put their trust in Him. To say that God foreknew us is to say He "foreloved" us (Acts 2:23; Rom. 8:29; 1 Pet. 1:1–2).

Glorification: The consummation of salvation. It occurs, in one sense, when we die and enter the presence of the Lord. At that point we will be completely free from the presence of sin. Glorification, however, occurs at its fullest when all who have died in Christ—as well as believers who are alive at Christ's return—will receive perfect, incorruptible bodies that will last for eternity. The process of sanctification will then be complete. We will be with Jesus and like Jesus—free from the presence of sin and perfect in body and soul (Rom. 8:23, 30; 1 Cor. 15:50–54; 1 John 3:2).

Gospel: The gospel, in a phrase, is "the joyous proclamation of God's redemptive activity in Christ Jesus on behalf of man enslaved by sin."[1] When we embrace the gospel by faith, we believe that Jesus lived and died for us, paying the penalty for our sins and providing us forgiveness; and that He was raised victoriously and bodily from the grave and lives for us today. All of this is motivated and accomplished by God's grace. This good news of salvation in Christ appears in the Old Testament in the form of promises, prophecies, and foreshadowing images (e.g., the promise of a redeemer in Genesis 3:15, the Passover lamb in Exodus 12, the prophecy of Christ's crucifixion in Isaiah 53, and the sacrificial system detailed in Leviticus). In the New Testament, the bright truth of the gospel bursts forth in all its glory. The four Gospels present the words and works of Christ. Acts chronicles the spread of the gospel in the known world, and the epistles explain the gospel and all its implications for

---

1. Robert H. Mounce, "Gospel," in *Evangelical Dictionary of Theology*, ed. Walter A. Elwell (Grand Rapids, Mich.: Baker Books, 1984), p. 472.

living the Christian life. And Revelation promises the consummation of our salvation, as Christ returns to claim His church. Not surprisingly, Paul used the word *gospel* some sixty times in his epistles. The message of salvation in Christ and all that means for living was the core of his message and mission (Rom. 1:15–17; 1 Cor. 15:1–4; Gal. 1:6–9; Phil. 1:12).

Grace: Unmerited favor freely granted to believers in Christ. When we say we're saved by grace, we mean that salvation comes to us, not by our ability to earn God's favor or live up to His standards, but by His free gift to us. Although salvation is a free gift, it cost God a great deal—the incarnation and death of His Son. One writer defined grace with the acrostic God's Riches At Christ's Expense.[2] Instead of receiving the judgment we deserve for our sin, we will spend an eternity in the blessed presence of our Lord. All because of grace (Rom. 5:15–17, 21; 6:14; Eph. 2:4–8; Titus 3:4–7).

Justification: God's declaration or pronouncement that sinners, upon believing in Christ, are righteous because of Christ—even though still in a sinning state (Rom. 3:23–24; Gal. 3:11). As such, we are assured of God's blessings toward us and need no longer fear His wrath or condemnation. Justification is an instantaneous act of God that begins the Christian life. Once justified (declared righteous), the Christian begins the process of sanctification (growing in Christ).

Law: God's moral demands on His created human beings. The Law reflects God's holy character and His purposes for the people He created. His Law is summarized in the Ten Commandments (Exod. 20:1–17) and more fully explained by Jesus in the Gospels (Matt. 5:21–22, 27–28) and by Paul and other New Testament writers. God's Law in the Old Testament included civil laws for the theocratic nation of Israel and ceremonial laws (sacrifices, kosher diet, etc.) that taught the need for moral purity. God still demands moral perfection from His human creatures. But unregenerate sinners cannot keep God's Law. They hate it, in fact. The Law exposes our sinfulness and our need for God's grace (Rom. 7:7). And that is the Law's main

2. As quoted by Ray C. Stedman in *Birth of the Body* (Santa Ana, Calif.: Vision House Publishers, 1974), p. 98.

purpose. It cannot make us righteous, but it drives us to Christ, who kept the Law perfectly and who clothes us with His own righteousness (Gal. 3:23–29). Once saved, Christians no longer hate the Law. They agree with God that His moral demands are good, and they strive to obey Him—not to earn salvation, but out of gratitude for salvation (Ps. 19:7–11; 119:35; Rom. 8:3–4; 12:1).

Predestination: In its wider sense, the word refers to God's predetermining whatever comes to pass—His working "all things after the counsel of His will" (Eph. 1:11b). In its narrower sense, which specifically relates to salvation, predestination refers to God's selecting out of sinful humanity a multitude of people He would save through Christ (Rom. 8:29; Eph. 1:4–6; see also Jer. 1:5). This narrower sense of predestination is also referred to as election. Election is closely related to foreknowledge but differs from it in that foreknowledge tells us God loved us in eternity past, whereas election tells us what that love accomplished—our salvation.

Propitiation: The satisfaction of God's wrath against sin through the sacrifice of His Son on the cross (Rom. 3:25–26). God is holy; humanity is sinful. Because God cannot excuse or condone sin, He must punish it. In His grace, He sent Jesus Christ to suffer His wrath in our place. Thus, the Cross upholds God's character as both a righteous Judge and a merciful Savior—the just One and the One who justifies (Rom. 3:26).

Righteousness: When applied to God, the word refers to His good, perfect, and holy nature and His ability to do only what is right. God cannot sin. He cannot condone sin. He cannot be unjust. And He cannot err. He always and in every way acts in accord with His perfect moral nature. When applied to humans, righteousness is what God demands of us in terms of how we live. He requires that we live in perfect obedience to His moral law— that we conform to it inwardly as well as outwardly. Since no one is able to do this (Paul says in Romans 3:10 that "there is none righteous, not even one"), someone must earn righteousness for us. That's what Jesus did. He lived a perfectly obedient life under the Law. His every thought, motive, action, and word was pleasing to the Father. Then He died on the cross to take the punishment for our *un*righteousness. When we put our trust in Jesus, His righteousness is imputed to us—that is, God counts us as righteous, even though we still sin . . . because Christ has given His righteousness to us. Believers grow in righteousness in this life but will never be perfectly righteous until heaven.

Salvation: God's delivering us from the penalty, power, and presence of sin. Immediately upon believing in Jesus, we are delivered from the penalty of sin (eternal damnation) and the power of sin (its mastery over our lives). When we finally see the Lord face-to-face, we will be free from the presence of sin. Salvation includes not only our souls but our bodies as well, which will be resurrected on the last day.

Sanctification: When we put our trust in Christ, we were made righteous *positionally;* God declared us righteous (justified us) because of the life and death of His Son. But justification also marks the beginning of sanctification—the process of our becoming righteous *practically,* being set apart to God by the Spirit to grow out of sin and more fully into Christ. We will never be perfectly sanctified until heaven, but we will move toward perfection. We will change. We will, by the power of the Holy Spirit, conform more and more to the will of God and live lives that are pleasing to Him (Rom. 6:19; 1 Thess. 4:3–7; 5:23). Sin will always be present with us in this life, but its influence over us will be lessened over time in the process of sanctification.

Sin: Sin is both a condition and an expression. We are sinful by nature, born corrupt (Ps. 51:5; Rom. 3:10–11; Eph. 2:1). And that condition naturally produces thoughts and actions that violate God's Law (Gal. 5:19–21). Salvation in Christ is the only way to escape God's wrath toward sin and enter a life in which sin no longer controls us. Christians have the assurance that we will be free once and for all from the presence of sin when we step out of this life and into the next.

Works: We can view human works in two ways. One is to see them as deeds performed to earn God's favor so that He will repay us with salvation. The Bible is very clear that such a system of salvation is futile, since none of us can live righteously enough to keep God's Law (Rom. 3:9–18, 20; Gal. 3:10). That is why we must trust in Christ, whose works were perfect under the Law (Rom. 3:21–26; 5:6–11; 2 Cor. 5:21; Heb. 4:15). The Christian, however, has a second way to view works: good works grow out of our new life in Christ (Rom. 6:1–2, 11–13; 8:29; Gal. 5:22–24; Eph. 2:8–10; James 2:14–26; 1 John 3:16–19; 4:19–21). Indwelled by God's Spirit and in gratitude for what Christ has done for us, Christians do deeds that are pleasing to Him. When we sin, however, we need to remember that our salvation is still secure and that we have forgiveness, thanks to the perfect lawkeeping and sacrificial death of Jesus.

ROMANS

THE GOSPEL...

	...Saving the Sinner	...Concerning Israel	...Concerning Christian Conduct
	Depravity of humanity Grace of God Justification by faith Sanctification through the Spirit Security of the saint	Divine sovereignty and human will Past, present, and future of the nation	Social Civil Personal
	CHAPTERS 1:18–8:39	*CHAPTERS 9–11*	*CHAPTERS 12:1–15:13*
Emphasis	Doctrinal	National	Practical
Response	Faith	Hope	Love
Doctrine of God	Wrath — Righteousness	Glory	Grace
Doctrine of Humanity	Fallen — Dead	Saved — Struggling	Freed
Doctrine of Sin	Exposed — Conquered	Explained	Forgiven
Scope	Dead in sin — Dead to sin	Peace with God	Love for others
Main Theme	God's righteousness is given to those who put their faith in Jesus Christ.		
Key Verses	1:16–17		

Chapter 1

THE CHRISTIAN'S CONSTITUTION

A *Survey of Romans*

Romans has been called a constitution and manifesto for believers, containing the essence of the Christian life. Though personal in tone, it is a well-developed presentation of grace-filled, God-exalting theology that beckons the mind to stretch, the heart to soar, and the soul to sing.

As we embark on a study of this grand letter, let this description of Romans from the *New Geneva Study Bible* prepare you for the exciting discoveries ahead.

> Romans is Paul's fullest, grandest, most comprehensive statement of the gospel. Its compressed declarations of vast truths are like coiled springs—once loosed, they leap through mind and heart to fill one's horizon and shape one's life. John Chrysostom, the fifth century's greatest preacher, had Romans read aloud to him once a week. Augustine, Luther, and Wesley, three supremely significant contributors to the Christian heritage, all came to assured faith through the impact of Romans. All the Reformers saw Romans as the God-given key to understanding

This chapter has been adapted from "Romans: Cornerstone of Christian Truth" in the study guide *God's Masterwork, Volume 4: Matthew–1 Thessalonians*, coauthored by Gary Matlack and Bryce Klabunde, from the Bible-teaching ministry of Charles R. Swindoll (Anaheim, Calif.: Insight for Living, 1997).

all Scripture, since here Paul brings together all the Bible's greatest themes. . . . From the vantage point given by Romans, the whole landscape of the Bible is open to view, and the relation of the parts to the whole becomes plain. The study of Romans is vitally necessary for the spiritual health and insight of the Christian.[1]

Background of Romans

To lay a foundation for understanding this life-changing letter, let's take some time to consider its place in the Bible, as well as the history behind it.

An Epistle from an Apostle

The apostle Paul's letter to the Romans marks the beginning of the section of the New Testament known as the Epistles or letters. These writings, Romans through Jude, follow and expand on the Gospels and Acts. The Epistles set forth the implications and out-workings of the Christian life. They also deal with a variety of issues crucial to the life of the church—doctrinal purity, organization and implementation of worship, relationships within and outside the church, suffering, persecution, heaven's hope, and so on.

Of the twenty-one epistles, Paul wrote thirteen. John wrote three, Peter wrote two, and James and Jude wrote one apiece. No one knows for sure who wrote Hebrews, although many scholars suggest it could very well be Paul's fourteenth letter.

Paul's Relationship with the Church in Rome

Paul did not establish the church in Rome, nor had he visited it at the time of his letter, though he was well aware of its growth and impact (see Rom. 1:8–13). It's likely that this church began shortly after Pentecost (see Acts 2), as Roman Jews returned from Jerusalem to their city with the fire of the gospel still burning in their hearts. The Good News then spread to Rome's vast Gentile population.

The Roman church was growing at the same time Paul was spreading the gospel of Christ in the east. By the time he wrote to the Romans, he had been evangelizing, planting churches, and

---

1. New Geneva Study Bible, gen. ed. R. C. Sproul, New Testament ed. Moisés Silva (Nashville, Tenn.: Thomas Nelson Publishers, 1995), pp. 1764–65.

training leaders from Judea to Macedonia for about ten years. The time had come for him to take the gospel to new territories.

So he set his sights on Spain. From the city of Corinth, he would go to Jerusalem, where he planned to deliver a monetary gift to the church there, then sail from Jerusalem to Spain. On the way he would stop at Rome, the capital of the Empire, to encourage the Christians there in their walk with Christ.

More Than a Correspondence—a "Constitution"

In Corinth, probably in the winter of A.D. 57, Paul dictated a letter to his personal scribe, Tertius, telling the Roman Christians about his plans. But this letter is no mere itinerary. Paul saw his correspondence as an opportunity to ground the Romans in the essentials of the faith, for the church there had no definitive statement of Christian truth. They needed a "constitution" to go by, not just so they could learn, but so they could be a light to the rest of the Empire.

Style and Theme

The letter unfolds in a logical, systematic fashion, as Paul presents in debate form his case that God provides for us what He requires of us—perfect righteousness. Through faith in Christ alone, a "righteousness from God" is imparted to sinners. Through Christ's atoning sacrifice, God removes His holy wrath toward us and brings us into loving relationship with Himself forever. That, in a couple of sentences, is the theme of Romans.

Survey of Romans

Before feasting on the rich truths of Romans verse-by-verse, let's feast our eyes on the whole banquet set before us. There are five main servings: an introduction (1:1–17), a doctrinal section (1:18–8:39); a national section (chaps. 9–11), a practical section (12:1–15:13), and a conclusion (15:14–16:27).

Introduction (1:1–17)

Paul begins by introducing himself and his mission. He is "a bond-servant of Christ Jesus, called as an apostle, set apart for the gospel of God" (1:1). His passion is to preach the gospel, for it is the "power of God for salvation to everyone who believes" (v. 16).

3

Then he acquaints us with his letter's main theme: the "righteousness of God" (v. 17). The term *righteousness*, which appears thirty-five times in Romans, is defined by Paul as inward and outward conformity to God's Law. And no one, he contends, can attain righteousness apart from divine intervention. The righteousness we need in order to please God must come from God Himself.

Doctrinal Section (1:18–8:39)

The bad news: We're all guilty (1:18–3:20). Paul has both good news and bad news for us. First, the bad news: "There is none righteous, not even one" (3:10). All humanity is corrupted by sin, unable to live according to God's perfect standards, and sitting in the crosshairs of God's judgment.

The good news: God has given us His righteousness (3:21–5:21). Now for the good news. Since sinful people can't possibly come to God on their own merits, He provided the way through His Son. Though we have all "sinned and fall[en] short of the glory of God" (3:23), we can be "justified as a gift by His grace through the redemption which is in Christ Jesus" (v. 24).

Justified is another key word for Paul. To be justified is to be declared righteous by God, even though we still struggle with sin in this life. Because we have placed our faith in Christ and are clothed in His perfect righteousness, God forgives and accepts us.

Justification by faith, Paul explains, isn't a new idea. Both Abraham (4:1–3) and David (vv. 6–8) were justified by faith. This certainly weakens the argument of legalists who claimed that Jews were and had always been saved by keeping the Law.

All people, Jews and Gentiles alike, have inherited a sinful nature from Adam (5:12). But, just as Adam's disobedience brought sin and death to humanity, Christ's obedience brings righteousness and life (vv. 18–19).

More good news: We don't have to live as we used to (chaps. 6–8). Salvation, rather than freeing us to sin, frees us to *not* sin (6:2–11). As believers in Christ, we are united with Him and His strength. Sin no longer has a claim on our lives. We're "alive to God in Christ Jesus" (v. 11).

The daily process of living this new life in Christ is called "sanctification" (see v. 22). Whereas justification is God's *declaration* of righteousness, sanctification is our *development* in righteousness. Justification has to do with our *position* in Christ. Sanctification is the *process* of becoming more like Christ.

Old habits die hard, though, as we all know. Even though we're new creatures in Christ and will one day be perfect, we retain the vestiges of our old, sinful nature in this life (chap. 7). All Christians who truly want to grow, therefore, will experience a struggle.

We don't, however, struggle alone. The Holy Spirit helps us in our struggle (chap. 8). We live in the Spirit, who frees us to love and serve Christ. The Spirit is not only our source of strength but a sign that our salvation is secure in Christ.

National Section (Chaps. 9–11)

Next Paul demonstrates his love for the Jewish nation, whose rejection of Christ and the gospel grieves his heart.

He explains that Israel's rejection is both a matter of God's sovereign choice (chap. 9) and Israel's stubbornness and self-righteousness (chap. 10).

God, however, still has plans for Israel, as Paul's vivid depiction of an olive tree assures us. Though unbelieving Jews have been "cut off" (11:24) from the olive tree (the community of the redeemed) and believing Gentiles have been grafted in, "all Israel" will one day be saved and grafted back in (v. 26). This divine plan causes Paul to praise God for His "unfathomable" ways (v. 33).

Practical Section (12:1–15:13)

Having laid out the truth of what Christ has done for us in the first eleven chapters, Paul, in his usual style, here turns his attention to how we live for Him.

He urges us to consider our lives a sacrificial offering of gratitude to God, who has set us free to serve Him (12:1). Rather than being "conformed" to the world, we're to be "transformed by the renewing of [our] mind[s]" (v. 2). And rather than dwelling on our own importance, we're to consider the value of others (vv. 3–8). We're to live in a way that serves and benefits others and combats evil with good (vv. 9–21).

The realm of civil government also takes on new meaning for the Christian. We're to pray for our leaders, submit to them, and live exemplary lives under their administration (chap. 13).

Life in Christ also brings freedom from the expectations and moral lists of others. Though we're all to be sensitive to and respect the convictions others hold, righteousness isn't defined by our participation or abstinence. "The kingdom of God," says Paul, "is not eating and drinking, but righteousness and peace and joy in the Holy Sprit" (14:17).

Pleasing ourselves isn't the goal of the Christian life either (15:1). We're to follow Jesus' example and work for the good of our neighbor, "accept[ing] one another, just as Christ also accepted us to the glory of God" (v. 7).

The Christian life is a different life. And all the resources we need to live it are found in Christ Himself.

Conclusion (15:14–16:27)

Paul wraps up his letter with a personal and pastoral tone. He encourages his readers that they have the abilities they need to live for Christ (15:14), reminds them of his mission (vv. 15–16), reveals his longing to see them (vv. 23–24), humbly asks for prayer (v. 30), and sends loving greetings (chap. 16).

His final words are what we would expect from a man who simply couldn't get over the grace and the greatness of God.

> To the only wise God, through Jesus Christ, be the glory forever. Amen. (16:27)

There you have it. A quick survey of the inspired feast set before us. The first course is coming right up.

✝ Living Insights

Romans is no light snack for the soul. It's a full-course meal meant to be savored over time. So don't just blitz through the kitchen, yank off a drumstick, and head out for soccer practice. Take some time. Sit down at the table. Anticipate the tastes. Enjoy the spicy aromas wafting out of the kitchen. Appreciate the presentation.

As you spread the white cloth napkin across your lap, what are you anticipating for this first volume of Romans? Perhaps you could read through the first five chapters of the epistle in one sitting and identify any personal issues you would like to address, theological questions you want to answer, or topics you might want to explore. Or, if you're really a connoisseur, you can outline the first five chapters of Romans. Feel free to use the chart at the beginning of the guide or a good study Bible to help.

What I Want to Get Out of Romans

_____

_____

_____

_____

_____

_____

_____

_____

_____

_____

_____

_____

_____

_____

_____

_____

_____

_____

_____

_____

Hungry? Let's dig in.

Chapter 2

MAY I INTRODUCE YOU TO THE GOSPEL?

Romans 1:1–17

$\mathbf{P}$aul.

A name. The first word in the book of Romans. You might not be surprised to find the great apostle's moniker so prominently positioned in his best-known work. Yet this is a mark of literary style, not Paul's desire for prominence. Writers in Paul's day didn't wait until the end of the letter to identify themselves but dispensed with mystery and gave their names at the beginning.

After reading just the first few verses of Romans, you'll see why Paul wasn't interested in making a name for himself. This letter isn't about him. It's about the God who called him. The Savior who loved him. Saved him. Changed him. Owned him. Romans is about the righteous and holy God who reaches down to sinful people and gives them life in His Son. Paul is the writer. But the story—and the glory—are God's.

Paul: The Man and His Mission

Paul opens his greeting to the Romans with these words:

> Paul, a bondservant of Christ Jesus, called as an apostle, set apart for the gospel of God. (Rom. 1:1)

Now there's a man who knows what he's about! Paul's identity and purpose are inextricably linked with the God who saved him and called him into service.

A Bondservant of Christ

Notice the terms Paul uses to describe himself. He's a "bond-servant" of Christ, a slave. All slaves have masters, and Paul's is Christ. Paul belongs to Christ, and he is committed to Him and His cause. This term also communicates a humility that puts Paul on the same level as his readers. No Christian, not even the great apostle, has any grounds for boasting in his or her position. No matter what recognition or responsibility comes our way, we are all servants of Christ.

And serving Christ is a good thing. Our Master is loving and benevolent, not abusive. He has rescued us from our old slavemaster, sin, and set us free to love Him and live in righteousness. We submit to Him out of joy, not from the threat of the whip. In calling himself Christ's "bondservant," Paul is "reveling in the Old Testament picture of a slave who in love binds himself to his master for life (Ex. 21:2–6)."[1]

Called as an Apostle

Paul also identifies himself as an "apostle." The word literally means "one who is sent." But its usual sense in Scripture is not so generic. It refers to

> an eyewitness of the Resurrection (Acts 1:22; 1 Cor. 15:8) who had been personally appointed by Christ (Matt. 10:1–7; Acts 1:24–26; Gal. 1:1) to govern the early church (1 Thess. 4:8; 2 Thess. 3:6, 14), and to teach or write with authority (1 Cor. 14:37; 1 Thess 2:13; 4:15; 2 Pet. 3:15, 16). The term is used as a title of the twelve disciples and Paul.[2]

Notice, though, that Paul has not sought the office of apostle. God "called" him to that position. He doesn't see his ministry as one of his own making or as a product of his own ambition. He, by God's grace, fits into God's plan. Not vice versa.

Set Apart for the Gospel

God has "set apart" Paul, which means He has separated him for a special purpose. And that purpose is to preach the good news of salvation in Christ.

So that's how Paul sees himself: as a humble participant whom God has graciously included in His grand purposes.

---

1. John A. Witmer, "Romans," in *The Bible Knowledge Commentary*, New Testament edition, ed. John F. Walvoord and Roy B. Zuck (Wheaton, Ill.: Scripture Press Publications, Victor Books, 1983), p. 440.

2. *New Geneva Study Bible*, gen. ed. R. C. Sproul, New Testament ed. Moisés Silva (Nashville, Tenn.: Thomas Nelson Publishers, 1995), p. 1828.

The Gospel: The Content of Paul's Message

Paul now moves from a description of his God-appointed role to a definition of his message. The gospel, he says, was

> promised beforehand through His prophets in the holy Scriptures. (Rom. 1:2)

Not a New Message

Contrary to what many of Paul's detractors have been saying, the gospel isn't some newfangled message opposed to Judaism. Rather, it actually has its roots there—and even more than that, it is the fulfillment of all the Jews had hoped for. The gospel appears in seed form throughout the Old Testament in promises of a coming Messiah; images like sacrifices and the temple; and pictures of Christ in the lives of prophets, priests, and kings. Salvation in Christ has been God's great plan from the very beginning.

Centered on the Son

> Concerning His Son, who was born of a descendant of David according to the flesh, who was declared the Son of God with power by the resurrection from the dead, according to the Spirit of holiness, Jesus Christ our Lord. (vv. 3–4)

These two verses are packed with important theology. They're not only a summary statement of the gospel, they're an affirmation of Christ's unique nature.

Jesus was both fully divine ("His Son," "Son of God," "Lord") and fully human ("a descendant of David according to the flesh"). This contradicts Gnosticism, on the one hand (which asserts that Jesus didn't have a real human body; it was only an illusion), and liberalism on the other (which says that Jesus was a good man, but He wasn't God). Jesus had to be both human and divine to purchase our salvation. Also, Jesus' descendancy from David confirms Old Testament prophecy that the Messiah would come from that king's line (see 2 Sam. 7:16; Isa. 9:7; 11:1–10; 16:5; Jer. 23:5–6; see also Matt. 1:1–17).

You can't have the gospel without Christ; the gospel *is* Christ. He is the promised Messiah; the eternal Son of God made flesh; the One who lived, died, and rose again so that we may have eternal life.

Not only is Jesus the content of Paul's message, He is the One who commissioned Paul to preach the gospel to the Gentiles (Rom. 1:5), which includes his Roman readers (v. 6). Having embraced Christ, they are loved by God and called by Him to be "saints" (or literally, "holy ones"). No wonder, then, Paul can greet them with grace and peace (v. 7). For salvation in Christ comes only by God's grace, and the only way to be at peace with God is through His Son.

Paul and the Roman Christians

Having identified himself, his mission, and his message in this minisermon of a greeting, Paul now turns his attention to his purpose for writing: to ground the Roman Christians in the gospel. In verses 8–15, we find that Paul has not only a passion for the gospel but a love for his fellow Christians in Rome and a desire to see them grow in their faith.

Thankfulness for Their Faith

> First, I thank my God through Jesus Christ for you all, because your faith is being proclaimed throughout the whole world. (v. 8)

Why does Paul thank the Christians in Rome? Have they sent him a gift? Supported his ministry? No, he's thankful for their renowned faith. This tells us something about Paul's priorities: He is grateful that people throughout the Roman empire are taking notice of the vitality and genuineness of the Christian life radiating from the Roman church. Notice, it wasn't the size of the church or its wealth or its busyness that excited Paul. It was the Romans' vibrant and steadfast faith.

What an encouragement to his own message and ministry this must have been! As we have mentioned, Paul had not planted the church in Rome, yet he is thankful for their reputation. To Paul, ministry is not about church competition but about making Christ known.

The believers in Rome have been confirming by their lives that Christ is real, that He is alive, and that the gospel is valid. From Rome—the seat of paganism, idolatry, materialism, and growing hostility toward Christianity—the light of Christ is burning bright enough for the whole empire to see.

Praying for a Visit

> For God, whom I serve in my spirit in the preaching
> of the gospel of His Son, is my witness as to how
> unceasingly I make mention of you, always in my
> prayers making request, if perhaps now at last by the
> will of God I may succeed in coming to you. (vv. 9–10)

Despite their good testimony, if they want to deepen in their
faith, the Roman Christians need further instruction in the gospel.
Which is why Paul has been praying for an opportunity to visit
them. He wants to impart "some spiritual gift"[3] to them, that is, to
minister to them in such a way that they are strengthened or "established" in their faith (v. 11). Paul also knows that he will benefit
from his time with the Romans because they will encourage one
another (v. 12).

Though other ministry duties have so far kept him from trav-
eling to Rome, Paul is anxious to "obtain some fruit among [the
Roman Christians]" as he has with other Gentiles (v. 13). This fruit
probably refers to the results God was producing in Paul's ministry—
namely, that Gentiles were coming to faith in Christ and growing
in Him.

A Gospel for All People

> I am under obligation both to Greeks and to bar-
> barians, both to the wise and to the foolish. (v. 14)

No wonder Paul's ministry is bearing fruit. He offers Christ's
message of redemption to all people. Salvation was and still is for
everyone—people of all ethnic groups, income and educational
levels, cultural distinctives, ages, and of both genders.

The Gospel for Believers?

The gospel is even for . . . believers? That's what Paul says next.

> So, for my part, I am eager to preach the gospel to
> you also who are in Rome. (v. 15)

---

3. It's best not to understand "spiritual gift" here in the usual sense of special enablement
and abilities (tongues, teaching, etc.) given to believers upon regeneration. The Holy Spirit,
not apostles, gives those. Paul is probably referring to using his own gifts to build up the
Roman Christians in their faith.

He's talking about the *Christians* in Rome—the "called of Jesus Christ" (v. 6), "beloved of God" (v. 7), and "saints" (v. 7). This may seem like a small point, but it's not. The gospel isn't just a "get saved now" message tacked on to the end of a sermon or conversation. The gospel is infinitely instructive. It's like a bottomless treasure chest. Just when we think we've gathered as much as we can, we find that we've only scraped off the first layer.

Christ lived, died, and rose again for sinful humanity. That's the gist of the gospel. And we can put our trust in Christ after hearing a simple message like that and be saved. But that's only the beginning. God not only saved us, He chose us in eternity past. We're united to Christ. He continues to work in us to His glory. We need no longer fear God's condemnation. We have a glorious future waiting for us. We can now love others as we should. These are all gospel truths, inexhaustible treasures that we all need in order to enrich our walk of faith.

The Power of the Gospel

With such glories of the gospel in mind, Paul's next words seem like a strange understatement:

For I am not ashamed of the gospel. (v. 16a)

Why would he be ashamed?

Proclamation amid Persecution

Well, let's think about the resistance and ridicule of the gospel that existed in Paul's day. The majority of Jews hated the Good News; it undermined their system of self-achieved righteousness. The Gentiles hated the gospel too—how dare these Christians teach that there's only one God? Paul reminds us elsewhere that the world sees the gospel as foolishness (see 1 Cor. 1:21–25).

So to stand strong in the midst of such opposing winds and declare the Good News of Jesus Christ wasn't—and isn't—always easy to do.

Power and Righteousness

Paul's point is that the gospel is nothing to be embarrassed about or hidden. For it is

the power of God for salvation to everyone who believes, to the Jew first and also to the Greek. For

in it the righteousness of God is revealed from faith
to faith; as it is written, "But the righteous man shall
live by faith." (vv. 16b–17)

The gospel has the power to do what we can't—save us, forgive
our sins, bring us into the family of God—because the gospel contains the righteousness of God. The NIV says "a righteousness *from*
God" (emphasis added), which is actually clearer. In Christ, God
gives us His own righteousness.

Some have called verses 16–17 the most important verses in
the Bible. Commentator James Montgomery Boice writes,

> They are the theme of this epistle and the essence
> of Christianity. They are the heart of biblical
> religion. . . . They tell how a man or woman may
> become right with God.[4]

Verse 17 is the verse that caused the great reformer Martin
Luther to realize that all his efforts to work his way to God had
been futile. In order for him to be accepted by God, he had to have
the very righteousness of God granted to him in Christ. And so do we.

Because of our inherent sinfulness, we can do nothing to save
ourselves. We cannot live good enough lives to meet God's require-
ments for perfect obedience. So God, in His mercy and love, has
clothed believers with the righteousness of His own Son. That is
how we become right with God. That's power. Real power.

This power comes only through faith in Christ. Salvation is
from "faith to faith," through-and-through a work of God granted
by faith, not human accomplishment. That's why God—not Paul
nor any other sinful human being—deserves all the glory.

☩ *Living Insights*

The righteousness of God granted to sinful people. This theme,
introduced in these first seventeen verses of Romans, threads
throughout the letter and holds it together like a drawstring. There's
another, underlying theme, though, that also makes its way through
the book: the sovereignty of God.

---

4. James Montgomery Boice, *Romans: Justification by Faith, Romans 1–4* (Grand Rapids,
Mich.: Baker Book House, 1991), vol. 1, p. 103.

Look at the prominence Paul gives it in these verses. Not only is salvation God's doing, but so is the placement of people into service to declare salvation. Also, with the birth, life, death, and resurrection of Jesus, God perfectly fulfilled all His prophecies about the coming Messiah. And Paul recognized that, if he were to come to Rome, it would be up to God to get him there.

Complete, perfect, divine control. That's what sovereignty is. But it's bigger than just this simple definition. It has all kinds of implications for how we live, how we view success and failure, how we make decisions. For now, though, why not take stock of your own view of God's sovereignty. Then, as you work your way through the rest of this letter to the Romans, you can adjust it, if you need to, based on what you learn.

Is God sovereign over everything—every event, person, circumstance—or just over salvation?

_____

_____

How does God's sovereignty relate to my free choices? Is He sovereign over those, too, or does my freedom override His sovereignty? Or are God's sovereignty and my freedom equal forces in determining my life's outcome?

_____

_____

_____

If God does control the outcome of everything, why live responsibly? Why walk in obedience? Why share the gospel? Why do anything?

_____

_____

_____

All right. Hold those thoughts. And be prepared to grapple with the topic of sovereignty as we continue our study of Romans.

Chapter 3

SINNERAMA IN PANORAMA
(PART 1)
Romans 1:18–25

*S*inner? Me? In danger of God's judgment? Those are pretty strong words, don't you think? I mean, I love my family. I've never cheated on my wife or abused my kids. I'm honest and hard-working. I don't embezzle money from my employer. I'm kind and helpful to my neighbors. I even donate a sizable chunk of my income to charity. What did I ever do to make God mad at me?"

Chances are, you've heard a response like that when you've engaged a friend, neighbor, or coworker in a discussion about the sinfulness of humanity and our need for the Savior. You may have even used similar words yourself. That's because we tend to look at sin much differently from the way God does.

We like to look at sin as only the really bad stuff; God sees it as anything—not just actions, but also thoughts and motives—that violates His Law, His standards for perfect living. We often describe sin solely in terms of errant, isolated actions. The Bible, though, tells us that sin is a congenital condition of the soul that permeates our whole life. We are by nature sinners who reject God and His Law; that is why we sin. And we often limit sin's definition to those things that hurt other people. Scripture shows us, however, that sin is any offense to our holy God—even if no one else knows about it.

Loving our families, being honest employees, donating to charities—these greatly benefit our communities and society as a whole. But such endeavors don't take away the problem of our inherent sinfulness. They can't bring God's forgiveness and remove His wrath. Only faith in Jesus Christ can do that.

The Dark Section of Romans

It isn't much fun to dwell on our sinfulness. But before thoroughly examining the Good News of salvation in Christ, Paul wants to make sure his readers understand their need for Him. That's why he takes a generous portion of the letter to paint a clear picture of the universal depravity of humanity (1:18–3:20). Yes, he is writing to Christians. But even Christians need to be reminded where we would be if Jesus Christ hadn't intervened. Without Christ, each and every person—from the vilest pagan to the most self-righteous religionist—stands condemned before God as a sinner. "There is none righteous," as Paul later writes, "not even one" (Rom. 3:10).

Beginning with 1:18–25, then, we'll be viewing the somber parade of human depravity. But remember, a breathtaking vista is just around the corner. The clear, fresh, bright presence of the gospel is on the way. The Son will come out. But to rejoice afresh in who Christ is, we must face the reality of what we would be without Him. After we have spent some time staring at the darkness of sin, then our hearts will bask in the dawn of His glorious grace.

The Wrath of God

We don't hear much about God's wrath these days, do we? Yet His wrath is just as much a part of His makeup as His love, mercy, power, and wisdom. Because of His perfectly good and holy nature, God cannot tolerate sin. He must judge it. He must respond to it in wrath.

In verses 1–17 of chapter 1, Paul introduced God's provision of righteousness, which comes through faith in Jesus Christ. Beginning in verse eighteen, he explains why we need a righteousness from God: because our inherent sinfulness separates us from God, keeps us from living a life pleasing to Him, and places us in the path of His wrath.[1]

Directed toward Sin

> For the wrath of God is revealed from heaven
> against all ungodliness and unrighteousness of men
> who suppress the truth in unrighteousness. (1:18)

God's wrath isn't like ours—a sudden, uncontrolled outburst of

---

1. Paul's inspired portrait of sinful humanity begins in 1:18 and ends at 3:20. Many commentators subdivide this section into condemnation of the Gentiles (1:18–32), condemnation of the Jews (2:1–3:8), and the universal condemnation of all people (3:9–20). This is a helpful way to approach this section, although Paul is clearer in some verses than in others as to whom he is describing (compare, for example, 2:1 and 2:17). There seems to be some overlap between subsections as to the sins characterized by Gentiles and Jews, but it's clear that Gentiles would have been characterized by idolatry and sexual perversion (1:18–32) and Jews by a "holier than thou" attitude and the Law (2:1–3:8). The most important truth to remember from this whole sin section is that without Christ, we all stand equally condemned before God (3:9–20).

anger that's saturated with sin. God's wrath is rooted in His goodness and holiness. The Greek word used here, *orgē*, can best be defined as "the settled and active opposition of God's holy nature to everything that is evil."[2] There will come a day when God will pour out His full wrath on those who have rejected Him (see Rev. 14:9–11; 20:11–15). Here, though, Paul is talking about God's ongoing and active disdain for sin.

This wrath is "revealed from heaven"—communicated by God to people through the Scriptures, the observable effects of sin that He allows, and the self-condemnation that arises from our consciences. These are all evidences of God's wrath.

The target of God's wrath is "all ungodliness and unrighteousness of men who suppress the truth in unrighteousness." We commit all manner of sins against God and one another, even when we know better. By doing this, we "suppress the truth"; we act contrary to the knowledge God has given us about Himself. We know what's right, but we prefer to sin.

No Excuses

Can we escape God's wrath by pleading ignorance? Can we argue, "Hey, I didn't know there was a holy God to whom I'm accountable"? Afraid not, says Paul. You see,

> that which is known about God is evident within them; for God made it evident to them. For since the creation of the world His invisible attributes, His eternal power and divine nature, have been clearly seen, being understood through what has been made, so that they are *without excuse*. (Rom. 1:19–20, emphasis added)

God's wrath doesn't come without reason. Everyone has evidence of God's existence and greatness but rejects His rule nonetheless. God is evident "within" us (v. 19). We are made in His image; we think, create, reason, feel, relate. We have a conscience, an innate sense of what is right and wrong.

God is also evident in "what has been made" (v. 20), that is, in His whole creation. This is what theologians call "general revelation."

---

2. Leon Morris, *The Epistle to the Romans* (1988; reprint, Grand Rapids, Mich.: William B. Eerdmans Publishing Co., 1992), p. 76.

We can't be saved by observing nature; salvation comes only through the gospel (special revelation). But in nature we can see evidence of God's great power, wisdom, and order. Since there's a creation, there must be a Creator. The psalmist wrote,

> The heavens are telling of the glory of God;
> And their expanse is declaring the work of His
> hands. (Ps. 19:1; see also Ps. 8)

Glittering stars flung across a black heaven. The earth in perfect orbit around the sun—close enough to sustain life but far enough away to keep from burning up. Sculpted mountains. The earth's crust carved into breathtaking canyons. Fish that glow in the blackest depths of the sea. A butterfly breaking free from a chrysalis. The meticulously spun web of a gray spider. Molecules, atoms, electrons. The growth of a child in the womb. Birth.

These all clearly attest to an almighty God who made everything, including us. Yet, even in the face of such evidence, we prefer to live life according to our own standards and for our own glory. And when people don't turn to the true God, they make their own gods—idols.

Replacing God with Idols

> For even though they knew God, they did not honor
> Him as God or give thanks, but they became futile
> in their speculations, and their foolish heart was
> darkened. Professing to be wise, they became fools,
> and exchanged the glory of the incorruptible God
> for an image in the form of corruptible man and of
> birds and four-footed animals and crawling creatures.
> (Rom. 1:21–23)

These verses lead some Bible scholars to believe that Paul is addressing primarily Gentiles in verses 18–32, since Gentiles worshiped multiple gods represented by images of humans and animals. He may have had the Roman and Greek cultures in mind here. But as we will see later in the letter, everyone—even the very religious Jews—were guilty of shaping God to their own liking. We all tend to substitute the true God with "idols" of some sort.

Sinful humanity knows that God exists, but we don't respond to this knowledge with worship or thanksgiving or praise. Instead, we use the intelligence God gave us to reduce the infinite God to finite images. God created us in His image, but we try to create a god according to our image, our preference.

Given Over to Sin

How, then, does God deal with such rebellion? Notice the repeated phrase, "God gave them over" (vv. 24, 26, 28). This phrase, commentator Everett F. Harrison tells us, means that "God simply took his hands off and let willful rejection of himself produce its ugly results in human life."[3] One way God judges, then, is to let sinners have their way. He allows sin to take its natural course until sinners will turn to Him for grace and mercy and rescue from destruction.

Given Over to Immorality

God first gives sinners over

> in the lusts of their hearts to impurity, so that their bodies would be dishonored among them. (v. 24)

The Greek word for *lusts* covers a wide range of illegitimate sexual activity. Commentator William Barclay defines the word, *epithumia*, as

> the passionate desire for forbidden pleasure. It is the desire which makes men do nameless and shameless things. It is the way of life of a man who has become so completely immersed in the world that he has ceased to be aware of God at all.[4]

Given Over to Idolatry

In Rome, of course, the pursuit of personal passion was king. And it's no mistake that this verse on sexual sin sits between two verses on idolatry (vv. 23, 25). Idolatry and sexuality were closely connected in the ancient world. Part of pagan worship involved visiting the temples of various deities and having sex with temple prostitutes. This, the worshipers believed, would bring pleasure to the gods and cause them to bless mortals. And Paul, remember, is

---

3. Everett F. Harrison, "Romans," in *The Expositor's Bible Commentary*, gen. ed. Frank E. Gaebelein (Grand Rapids, Mich.: Zondervan Publishing House, Regency Reference Library, 1976), vol. 10, p. 24.

4. William Barclay, *The Letter to the Romans*, rev. ed., The Daily Study Bible Series (Philadelphia, Pa.: Westminster Press, 1975), pp. 28–29.

writing this letter form Corinth, which lay in the shadow of the temple of Aphrodite, the goddess of love and beauty. It is said that this temple alone employed a thousand prostitutes.[5]

Such practices "dishonored" the participants' bodies, using them in a way God never intended, perverting His beautiful gift of sexuality. Also, by engaging in such detestable practices, these people

> exchanged the truth of God for a lie, and worshiped and served the creature rather than the Creator, who is blessed forever. Amen. (v. 25)

Perversion passed off as piety. Mythology substituted for theology. Wickedness instead of worship. Calling lies the truth, and fantasy, reality. Making God according to our image. May God preserve us from such things . . . and from the judgment they bring. May our love of Christ be our strongest passion, and devotion to Him our highest goal.

⌐⌐ Living Insights

Idolatry may seem passé, but it's actually alive and well, even among educated people, as the writers of the Life Application Bible Commentary point out:

> How can intelligent people turn to idolatry? Idolatry begins when people reject what they know about God. Instead of looking to him as the Creator and sustainer of life, they see themselves as the center of the universe. They soon invent gods that are convenient projections of their own selfish plans and decrees. These gods may be wooden figures, or they may be things we desire—such as money, power, or comfort. They may even be misrepresentations of God himself—a result of making God in their image, instead of the reverse. The common denominator is this: Idolaters worship the things God made

---

5. Donald H. Madvig, "Corinth," in The International Standard Bible Encyclopedia, rev. ed., gen. ed. Geoffrey W. Bromiley (1979; reprint, Grand Rapids, Mich.: William B. Eerdmans Publishing Co., 1988), vol. 1, p. 773.

rather than God himself. It is a tendency that we must constantly watch for in ourselves.[6]

An idol doesn't have to be a figure on your mantle that you pray to or burn incense to. It can be a mental distortion of God, an unbiblical concept of God. And most people who promote the worship of idols don't call them idols. They simply lure people into worshiping a god, for example, of prosperity theology, who wants everyone to be rich. Or a god who is merely a cosmic force, a part of nature. Or a god you can work your way to apart from grace, by doing all the right things.

That's why it's so important to build our understanding of God around the Scriptures. It is there, in God's own Word to us, that He has revealed Himself and offered us life in His Son. The Scriptures make the unknowable God knowable, the unseen God seen, the distant God near.

What's shaping your perspective of God these days? His Word or something else?

_____

_____

What, if anything, can you identify in your life that might be luring your worship and devotion away from the true God?

_____

_____

_____

_____

_____

_____

_____

_____

6. Bruce B. Barton, David R. Veerman, and Neil Wilson, *Romans,* in the Life Application Bible Commentary series (Wheaton, Ill.: Tyndale House Publishers, 1992), p. 30.

What steps can you take to correct your perspective? Studying through Romans is a great start, by the way. So is reading through a good book on systematic theology.

_____

_____

_____

_____

_____

_____

_____

How about your church? Is the pastor studying and preaching rich biblical truth and uplifting the character and nature of God? If not, what would you like to see change?

_____

_____

_____

_____

_____

_____

_____

From time to time, we all let people, possessions, and passions slip into God's rightful place. But thank God for His Son, Jesus Christ, who received God's wrath for the sin of idolatry and all other sins—past, present, and future. If we have trusted His Son, we need not fear His wrath.

Chapter 4
SINNERAMA IN PANORAMA
(PART 2)
Romans 1:26–32

M om . . . Dad . . . I'm gay. But it's OK. I'm convinced that
this is how God made me. I've accepted it. I have embraced
my homosexuality. And so should you."

How many families have been thrown into turmoil with words
like these? When a person "comes out of the closet," a flood of
emotion-filled questions and concerns comes rushing out as well.

"Wasn't I a good enough parent? Did I do something wrong?"

"Where do we go from here? What's the best way to continue
loving our child while disapproving of the lifestyle?"

"Or should I disapprove at all? Could it be that God actually
intended homosexuality as a legitimate way to express intimacy?
Or is it sin, as I have always believed?"

Well, these final verses of Romans 1 should remove any doubt
that homosexuality is sin and that it violates God's design for sexual
intimacy. Get ready, though. Because homosexuality isn't the only
sin Paul lists as evidence of humanity's depravity. Everyone who
gossips, deceives, even fails to love, is guilty before Him. In other
words, every one of us.

So hang on as Paul continues to tell us more about ourselves
than most of us want to know. Remember, though, while you're
standing knee-deep in all this sin, that sin doesn't have the last
word. Christ's gospel does.

God "Gave Them Over"

In our previous chapter, we learned that the very sins we commit, while grieving the heart of God, are also used by Him as a
form of judgment—remember the phrase "God gave them over"
(1:24, 26, 28). To show us just how damaging sin can be, and in
order to make it clear how much we need His grace, God will turn
us over to our sins.

We've already seen how God turned pagans over to their sexual
misconduct and idolatry (vv. 24–25). Beginning in verse 26, Paul
gets even more specific about how they twisted and corrupted the

beautiful gifts God gave them—such as sexual intimacy—to satisfy their appetite for sin . . . and how God turned them over to that sin as well.

Given Over to Homosexuality

> For this reason God gave them over to degrading passions; for their women exchanged the natural function for that which is unnatural, and in the same way also the men abandoned the natural function of the woman and burned in their desire toward one another, men with men committing indecent acts and receiving in their own persons the due penalty of their error. (vv. 26–27)

"For this reason" takes us back to verse 25, which describes idolatry. God gave people over to homosexuality because they were involved in idolatry, following gods of their own making. This is not surprising. Once the true God (and reverence for Him) is out of the picture, everything becomes permissible—including sexual perversion. If we can create a god to our liking, then we can create a life to our liking, free of any moral restraint.

The life of sin is a downward spiral, with one sinful practice leading to another. And God will often allow us to continue plummeting spiritually to show us just how far from Him we can fall.

Verses 26–27 also connect with verse 24, since that verse also addresses sexual sin. There Paul said that God gave people over to "the lusts of their hearts to impurity." This phrase most likely suggests fornication—sex outside of marriage in some form, be it premarital sex, cheating on a spouse, prostitution, and so forth.

But here, in describing homosexual activity, Paul uses the terms "unnatural" (v. 26) and "abandoned the natural" (v. 27). Homosexuality is not only a sin (as is other sexual sin); it is an *unnatural* sin. It violates God's basic design for sexual activity.

How different from what we hear in today's culture. Prime-time sitcoms, popular celebrities, politicians and legislators, and even some churches elevate lesbianism and male homosexuality to a legitimate lifestyle—every bit as natural as heterosexual intimacy. But the Scriptures tell us something different.

The Bible is clear in its pronouncement of homosexuality as sin (see Lev. 18:22; 1 Cor. 6:9). It's not the only sin. Nor is it an unforgivable sin. And heterosexual sinners are no more righteous in God's sight than homosexual sinners. But homosexual behavior is sin, nonetheless.

Some homosexuals have no desire to change. Others, though, may want to, but the drive is so strong that they believe it's useless to try. That's why acknowledging homosexuality as sin is the first step to change. Since it is sin, it is something that can be forgiven in Christ. It is a sin He died for. And it is a condition from which He can set people free. That doesn't mean that giving up the homosexual lifestyle will be easy—any easier than a heterosexual giving up a sexual addiction. But it does mean that giving it up is possible.

Continuing to practice homosexuality, though, will result in "due penalty" (Rom. 1:27). Homosexuality, like all sin, will produce destructive consequences if it is allowed to run its course.

Given Over to a Depraved Mind

Paul next explains that people rejected God, not only in their actions, but also in their thinking.

> And just as they did not see fit to acknowledge God any longer, God gave them over to a depraved mind, to do those things which are not proper. (v. 28)

Commentator John Murray explains that by not seeing fit to acknowledge God, people were really

> refusing to have God in their knowledge. The thought is that they did not deem God fit to have in their knowledge. The godlessness of the state of mind is apparent—they did not cherish the knowledge of God because they did not consider God worthy of such thought and attention.[1]

The writers of the *Life Application Bible Commentary* on Romans further clarify Paul's meaning:

> Humans sat in judgment on God to decide whether he fit the qualifications of a God that would be to their liking; they decided he did not meet those qualifications and so dismissed him from their lives.

1. John Murray, *The Epistle to the Romans* (Grand Rapids, Mich.: William B. Eerdmans Publishing Co., 1997), p. 49.

They had the knowledge (they were not ignorant),
but they did not want to use it.[2]

So, as judgment, God "gave them over" to the very condition He abhorred—a depraved, corrupt, perverted mind; a mind set on anything and everything but the holy and righteous Lord. He allowed their rejection of Him to run its course. Godless thinking, then, turned into godless living: "things which are not proper."

The Whole Spectrum of Sin

Paul isn't vague about the "things which are not proper." He follows that general phrase with a specific list of twenty-one sins—evidence of a depraved life that grows out of a depraved mind.

> Being filled with all unrighteousness, wickedness, greed, evil; full of envy, murder, strife, deceit, malice; they are gossips, slanderers, haters of God, insolent, arrogant, boastful, inventors of evil, disobedient to parents, without understanding, untrustworthy, unloving, unmerciful. (vv. 29–31)

Scholars have attempted to group these sins into some sort of orderly arrangement. It's probably best, though, to see the list as a representation of sin's extent and variety, not a systematic classification. Paul, after all, devised other "sin lists" that contain vices not repeated here in Romans (see 1 Cor. 6:9–10; Gal 5:19–21; Col. 3:5). Paul was well acquainted with the sinful practices of the nations of his day—as well as his own sinfulness.

Paul's purpose, then, is not to list every conceivable sin that humans commit, but to show that those who have rejected God display all manner of sinfulness.

Notice that these sins range from what we would call small or common sins (gossip, boastfulness, disobedience to parents) to heinous crimes (murder). This not only tells us the many forms sin takes, but it also reminds us that all sin is sin. Anything that violates God's standards of perfect obedience puts us in the path of His judgment.

It's not only a sin to murder someone, it's a sin to fail to love God or our neighbor as God wants us to love (compare Matt. 22:34–40).

---

2. Bruce B. Barton, David R. Veerman, and Neil Wilson, *Romans*, Life Application Bible Commentary Series (Wheaton, Ill.: Tyndale House Publishers, 1992), p. 36.

Earlier, we addressed the topic of homosexuality. It is sin. But what if we fail to extend mercy to a homosexual dying of AIDS? Or think that we're inherently more righteous just because we're hetero-sexual? Being "unmerciful" and "arrogant" are sins too.

You see, none of us gets off the hook. We all commit deeds that fall somewhere along the wide spectrum of sinfulness. We sin by doing things we shouldn't and by not doing things we should. We sin against God. We sin against our neighbors, who are created in His image. We sin with regard to what we possess and what we don't possess. We sin in our thoughts, desires, emotions, speech, and actions. We even sin by approving the wrong that others do (Rom. 1:32).

Without Christ and the righteousness He gives us through faith, we could never stand before God. We could never live lives that please Him. We would be forever lost in our sin. And that's what salvation is all about. When we believe in Jesus Christ, His righ-teousness covers all our sins. We escape eternal death, which is God's due punishment for sin (v. 32). And we step out of sin's death grip into the Lord's loving hands.

Which would you rather be? Given over to sin? Or given eternal life in Christ? Seems like a pretty clear choice. Have you made it?

⊤ Living Insights

Since homosexuality is as out in the open as it is today, there's a good chance you know someone who's caught up in this sin. Someone you care about. Someone you love. Someone whose life-style bears the marks of being "given over" to his or her sin.

Let's suppose you get the opportunity to engage this person in discussion about his or her sin and the forgiveness that's found in Christ? What are your worries, fears, hesitations, and discomforts about such a discussion?

_____

_____

_____

_____

_____

Is there anything from this chapter that could help you prepare for such an encounter? (Hint: Include yourself as part of sinful humanity rather than looking at all heterosexuals as righteous and all homosexuals as unrighteous; admit that we're all guilty before God.)

_____

_____

_____

_____

_____

How would you respond to the argument that God made homosexuals the way they are, and that homosexuality is not a sin? What Bible passages would you consult in order to clearly show homosexuality as sin (start with Lev. 18:22; Rom. 1:26–27; 1 Cor. 6:9)?

_____

_____

_____

_____

_____

This may be as far as you get. But if this individual truly wants to be free from the homosexual lifestyle, what passages would you share to offer the hope of the gospel (see Rom. 3:21–26; 5:1–2; 1 Cor. 6:9–11; Eph. 2:1–10)?

_____

_____

_____

No matter how this person responds, you have done the most loving thing you can. You have shared the truth about the only way we can be set free from sin—through faith in Jesus Christ. If the person does come to faith in Christ, that doesn't mean all the urges and temptations will go away. He or she will need the support of a good Bible-believing church—a congregation that doesn't skimp on truth but has the compassion and perseverance to help a person recover over the long haul. Why not make a list of churches and individuals you would like this person to be connected with should they come to faith.

_____

_____

_____

_____

_____

And what are you willing to do to help this person walk with God and abandon the old lifestyle?

_____

_____

_____

_____

_____

_____

_____

_____

_____

_____

_____

Chapter 5

JUDGMENT FOR THE JUDGMENTAL

Romans 2:1–16

See if you can identify what's wrong with the following fragments of conversation:

- "I can't stand Phil. You know why? He's always criticizing other people."

- "HEY! YOU KIDS KEEP IT DOWN! YOU'RE TOO LOUD! YOU'RE ALWAYS TOO LOUD! WHY CAN'T YOU LOWER YOUR VOICES AND TALK SOFTLY LIKE THE REST OF US!"

- "Isn't that Jennifer over there? Can you believe it? She's having a glass of wine with dinner (*munch*). Doesn't she know that her body is a temple of the Holy Spirit (*crunch, stuff*)? Why, she's defiling the temple (*gulp*). That stuff's poison. Hey, are you going to eat the rest of your chicken-fried double-bacon western hickory cheeseburger? I will if you don't. And I don't know about you (*chomp, chomp*), but two baskets of cheese fries just isn't enough for me. Hey, pass me the rest of that Death-by-Fudge Cake, would you? Waiter (*belch*), another Monster Malt, please! Man, I love this place."

Did you catch it? We all do it, don't we? When it comes to judging others, we're mighty quick on the draw; we're always ready with a hair-trigger accusation. But when it comes to noticing (and working on) our own shortcomings, we're slower than a snail on ice. And more often than not, we're guilty of the very sins we're criticizing.

Call it what you want. Self-righteousness. Hypocrisy. Spiritual pride. Living with blind spots. Failure to take the plank out of our own eye before pointing out the speck in another's. Whatever label we slap on it, it doesn't do what we think it does. It doesn't make us any better than anyone else. We don't become righteous by pointing out the sins of others. In fact, by judging others, we actually pronounce judgment on ourselves.

The guilt of the holier-than-thou club is Paul's focus in Romans 2:1–16. Let's turn our attention to that chapter and see why that's a club we don't want to be part of.

Guilty Judges

> Therefore you have no excuse, everyone of you who passes judgment, for in that which you judge another, you condemn yourself; for you who judge practice the same things. (2:1)

Gentiles or Jews?

To whom is Paul talking here? We know they're moralistic, judgmental of others. And "therefore" ties us back to the list of sins in 1:18–32. So it's obvious that these people would readily condemn those who commit such sins. But in passing judgment, they obviously don't consider themselves in the same class as those sinners.

Who are they specifically, however? Some commentators suggest that Paul is transitioning from a description of Gentile sins (1:18–32) to those of the Jews (2:1–3:8). Paul, however, doesn't seem to single out the Jews until 2:17. Plus, he mentions Jews and Gentiles together in verses 9–11. Paul might very well be addressing all moralists—self-righteous people who don't consider themselves sinners, be they Jew or Gentile.

In Judging Others, They Judge Themselves

Their self-evaluation, however, is inaccurate. They are without excuse (2:1). There is no justification for their passing judgment on others. Why? Because, whether they admit it or not, they are practicing the same things. They participate in what they condemn. Therefore, they condemn themselves.

Amazing, isn't it, how we can condemn bad behavior in others while practicing the same things ourselves? As fallen creatures, we are congenitally blind to our own faults. And we conveniently forget our own wrongdoing. Or we rationalize it. Or rename it.

- "Oh, I'm not argumentative or divisive," we reason. "I just have strong convictions."

- "Me? An anger problem? No way. I'm just enthusiastic."

- "Come on, that's not lying. That's salesmanship; part of doing business."

- "Pornography? Don't be ridiculous. I'm just, uh, appreciating art."

Rationalizing or renaming sin, however, doesn't change the fact that it's still sin. And sin brings God's righteous judgment.

And we know that the judgment of God rightly falls upon those who practice such things. But do you suppose this, O man, when you pass judgment on those who practice such things and do the same yourself, that you will escape the judgment of God? (vv. 2–3)

We cannot expect God to judge others and then overlook our guilt when we commit the same sins. Just because we're righteous in our own eyes doesn't mean we are in God's. And just because the judgment doesn't come immediately does not mean that it's not going to come at all.

God's Patience Has a Purpose

When we judge others while considering ourselves exempt from God's judgment, we are impugning His kindness.

Or do you think lightly of the riches of His kindness and tolerance and patience, not knowing that the kindness of God leads you to repentance? (v. 4)

What does it mean to "think lightly" of God's kindness, tolerance, and goodness? Commentator John Stott captures the essence of Paul's words.

Sometimes, in a futile attempt to escape the inescapable, namely God's judgment, we take refuge in a theological argument. For theology can be turned to bad uses as well as good. We appeal to God's character, especially to the riches of his kindness, tolerance and patience (4a). We maintain that he is much too kind and longsuffering to punish anybody, and that we can therefore sin with impunity. We even misapply Scripture to our advantage and quote such statements as, "The Lord is compassionate and gracious, slow to anger, abounding in love" [Ps. 103:8; Exod. 34:5]. But this kind of manipulative theologizing is to show contempt for God, not honour. It is not faith; it is presumption. For God's kindness leads us towards repentance (4b). That is its goal. It is intended to give us space in which to repent, not to give us an excuse for sinning [see also 2 Pet. 3:9].[1]

1. John Stott, Romans: God's Good News for the World (Downers Grove, Ill.: InterVarsity Press, 1994), pp. 82–83.

God's restraint of judgment shouldn't be taken as permission to sin or as His apathy toward wrongdoing. He is giving sinners time to come to Him and receive His forgiveness in Christ. But His patience doesn't last forever.

Judgment and Blessing

What happens to those who continue to disregard God's kindness and continue in sin?

> But because of your stubbornness and unrepentant heart you are storing up wrath for yourself in the day of wrath and revelation of the righteous judgment of God, who will render to each person according to his deeds: to those who by perseverance in doing good seek for glory and honor and immortality, eternal life; but to those who are selfishly ambitious and do not obey the truth, but obey unrighteousness, wrath and indignation. (vv. 5–8)

Those who choose a life of sinful self-righteousness and don't turn to Christ will suffer God's ultimate and eternal punishment. Those who embrace Christ by faith will receive eternal life. That's the plain and simple truth. Not one sin escapes the righteous wrath of God. Sin is always paid for—either by Christ, who was punished for our sins . . . or by the sinners who reject Him and suffer eternal punishment.

Salvation by Works?

Notice that Paul says God will judge each person "according to his deeds." Wait a minute! Doesn't salvation come by faith alone? Absolutely. None of us lives a perfect life, not even Christians. If our escaping God's judgment depends on our righteous deeds, we're all doomed. So Paul's phrase merits some explanation.

Salvation is a free gift from God. No one can be saved by just trying to live a better life. We cannot merit eternal life by our own works (see Rom. 3:20; Gal. 3:11; Eph. 2:8–9; Titus 3:4–7). Yet both the Old and New Testaments consistently speak of judgment according to works (Ps. 62:12; Jer. 32:19; Hos. 12:2; Matt. 16:27; 2 Cor. 5:10). How are these two truths compatible?

The answer is that true faith produces good works. As Paul wrote to the Ephesians, "We are His workmanship, created in Christ

Jesus for good works which God prepared beforehand so that we would walk in them" (Eph. 2:10). Our good works are evidence that we belong to Christ. That doesn't mean we stop sinning when we come to Christ. But it does mean that we will live in a way that identifies us as His own (see also James 2:14–26).

No Partiality with God

Our life's pattern, then, reveals where our hearts are (see Matt. 7:17–18). And if our hearts are selfishly ambitious and antagonistic toward the truth, that shows that they aren't aligned with God. Paul can't offer a happy ending in such a situation:

> There will be tribulation and distress for every soul of man who does evil, of the Jew first and also of the Greek, but glory and honor and peace to everyone who does good, to the Jew first and also to the Greek. For there is no partiality with God. (Rom. 2:9–11)

Why does Paul use the phrases "of the Jew first and also of the Greek" (v. 9) and "to the Jew first and also to the Greek" (v. 10)? Is he suggesting that the Jew has some sort of advantage in salvation or disadvantage in judgment compared to the Gentile? Not at all. He makes it very clear that Jews are no more inherently righteous before God than Gentiles and stand equally condemned as sinners before Him (2:17–29; 3:9–18).

Paul does, however, see the Jews as a privileged people to whom God has given His covenant and His Scriptures (3:1–2; 9:4–5). Also, the gospel came first to the Jews, then spread to the Gentiles. Both Jesus and Paul took the message of the Cross to their own people first (see Matt. 10:5–6; Acts 1:8; 13:46–47). Thus, Paul sees the Jews as having a greater responsibility to respond to the gospel. That's probably why he mentions the Jew first in the context of both salvation and condemnation (see also Rom. 1:16).

Paul's bottom line is that God's standards are the same for everyone, whether Jew or Gentile. It is whether we have put our faith in Christ that determines our eternal fate—not nationality, gender, position, or any other quality.

The Law as the Standard

How can God's assessment of our lives be fair? Because His perfect standard, the Law, is the great equalizer. It judges everyone the same—the Jews, who received the written Law, and the Gentiles, who possess a sense of right and wrong even without the written Law.

> For all who have sinned without the Law will also perish without the Law, and all who have sinned under the Law will be judged by the Law; for it is not the hearers of the Law who are just before God, but the doers of the Law will be justified. For when Gentiles who do not have the Law do instinctively the things of the Law, these, not having the Law, are a law to themselves, in that they show the work of the Law written in their hearts, their conscience bearing witness and their thoughts alternately accusing or else defending them, on the day when, according to my gospel, God will judge the secrets of men through Christ Jesus. (vv. 12–16)

The Jews received the Mosaic Law at Sinai, and it clearly detailed for them the way to live. Even for Jews in Paul's day, the reading of the Law was a regular part of synagogue worship. Having the Law, however, doesn't make one righteous. Only keeping it perfectly does. And no one but Christ has done that.

The Gentiles, on the other hand, were not the custodians of the Mosaic Law. But they did have God's Law "written in their hearts"—that is, they possessed a conscience, a sense of right and wrong, which they knew instinctively. And they couldn't even keep that moral code perfectly.

None of us can. No matter where we were born, where we grew up, what kind of family we had. Whether we had exposure to the Word of God or not. Apart from Christ, we all stand condemned by God's Law. As Paul will tell us later, "There is none righteous, not even one" (Rom. 3:10).

Just as the Law levels the playing field, judging all people equally, so the gospel levels the field, saving all who abandon their self-righteousness and put their trust in Jesus Christ.

Condemning others' sins may make us feel good about ourselves. It may make us feel superior to those around us whose faults are so obvious to us. But don't be fooled. Self-righteousness only heaps condemnation on our own heads. To obtain true righteousness, we must first see our own sinfulness . . . then run to Christ. For He not only removes the log from our eye, He removes the stain of sin from our lives.

✝ *Living Insights*

The idea of "judging others" is often misunderstood, prompting some people to conclude that we should never make a moral decision about anyone. But is that what it means? Let's explore this topic a bit further.

Start by reading Matthew 7:1–5. What is Jesus saying here? Is He saying we should never confront anyone about legitimate sin in their life? Or is He saying that spiritual introspection is necessary *before* spiritual confrontation?

_____

_____

_____

_____

_____

The study note on this passage from the *New Geneva Study Bible* states,

> Jesus prohibits one kind of judging, but approves a different kind. Condemning others for their faults is failure to exercise forgiveness (6:14, 15); only a gentle and humble criticism that first recognizes one's own greater faults can help.[2]

From the following Scripture passages, what forms of judgment are legitimate?

1 Timothy 3:1–7; Titus 1:5–9 _____

_____

_____

---

2. *New Geneva Study Bible*, gen. ed. R. C. Sproul, New Testament ed. Moisés Silva (Nashville, Tenn.: Thomas Nelson Publishers, 1995), p. 1515.

Matthew 7:6 _____

_____

_____

Matthew 10:16 _____

_____

_____

Matthew 18:15–20; 1 Corinthians 5:9–13 _____

_____

_____

With what kind of spirit are we to evaluate or confront others (see Gal. 6:1)?

_____

_____

_____

Self-righteous condemnation has no place in the spiritual life.[3] We would all be hopelessly lost in our sin if Christ had not saved us.

So that's the kind of judgment we're to avoid. Before we engage in any type of evaluation, assessment, or confrontation of others, we need to take a close look at the sins we're struggling with. Then we can move ahead with humility instead of a "holier than thou" attitude.

---

3. For an example of how much God hates self-righteousness, see Jesus' scathing rebuke of the Pharisees in Matthew 23:1–36.

Chapter 6

RELIGIOUS . . . BUT LOST

Romans 2:17–29

Ever since Romans 1:18, Paul has been bringing two groups of humanity before the bench of God's judgment. And the verdicts have rolled down with frightful certainty. Flagrant sinners? Guilty. People who think they're morally upright and who condemn flagrant sinners? Guilty.

Can *anyone* claim to live a righteous life before God? How about the Jews? After all, God gave them His Law. As scribes and teachers of holy writ, they had the very words of God in their possession. Surely the Jews, who held the Law in such high regard and urged others to do likewise, could claim a righteous standing before God.

Let's see how Paul addresses this question in 2:17–29, as we continue to examine the disturbing but inescapable truth of human depravity.

How the Jews Assessed Themselves

Paul knew exactly how most first-century Jews would have assessed themselves. He, after all, was a Jew who had at one time trusted in his own righteousness (see Phil. 3:4–6). So, anticipating that many of the Jews in Rome would have balked at the idea of being considered as sinful as the rest of humanity, he begins,

> But if you bear the name "Jew" and rely upon the Law and boast in God, and know His will and approve the things that are essential, being instructed out of the Law, and are confident that you yourself are a guide to the blind, a light to those who are in darkness, a corrector of the foolish, a teacher of the immature, having in the Law the embodiment of knowledge and of the truth . . . (Rom. 2:17–20)

A Privileged People

That's how the Jews saw themselves. Favored by God. Religious. Knowledgeable about the Scriptures. Models of morality. Commentator James Montgomery Boice divides the claims Jews made for themselves into two main categories—spiritual advantages and religious privileges. Each category contains four claims.

The claims having to do with the Jews' spiritual advantages are:

1. God has given us his law.

2. He has entered into a special relationship with us.

3. Because we have been given his law, we know his will, and

4. We approve only the most excellent of human moral standards.

The claims having to do with their privileges are:

1. To be a guide for the blind,

2. To be a light for those who are in the dark,

3. To be an instructor for the foolish, and

4. To be a teacher of infants.[1]

The first category deals with the Jews' relationship to God. The second encompasses their responsibility to others in light of that relationship. Quite a list! And we must, in one sense, agree with it. God did indeed choose Israel to be His covenant people. He gave them His Law at Sinai, something else no other nation could claim. And He called them to live holy lives and to be a light to the nations.

Does Privilege Guarantee Righteousness?

But the question is, Does the possession of such privileges and advantages guarantee a righteous life? Is *having* the Law the same as *living* the Law? No. In fact, greater privilege brings greater responsibility (see Luke 12:48). Greater knowledge brings greater accountability to act on that knowledge (see John 3:10; James 3:1). And the Jews, as Paul tells us next, even with all they had been given, stood condemned and in need of Christ—just like the rest of humanity.

---

1. James Montgomery Boice, *Romans, Volume 1: Justification by Faith (Romans 1–4)* (Grand Rapids, Mich.: Baker Book House, 1991), pp. 250–51.

How God Assessed the Jews

No doubt, self-righteous Jews would have read Romans 2:17–20 with a sense of satisfaction and pride, thinking perhaps that Paul was going to congratulate them for being the sole remnant of humanity who didn't fall under God's judgment and who were uniquely qualified to lead others in righteousness. But he throws them a curve.

> You, therefore, who teach another, do you not teach yourself? You who preach that one shall not steal, do you steal? You who say that one should not commit adultery, do you commit adultery? You who abhor idols, do you rob temples? You who boast in the Law, through your breaking the Law, do you dishonor God? For "the name of God is blasphemed among the Gentiles because of you," just as it is written. (vv. 21–24)

Ouch! As one writer put it, Paul's words are "a pricking of the balloon of Jewish pride and presumption."[2] The Jews possessed and taught the Law . . . and they were breaking it. They not only failed to practice what they preached; they did the exact opposite of what they preached.

In pointing out their sins, Paul focuses particularly on three violations of the Law: stealing, adultery, and idolatry. As commentator John Murray points out,

> The apostle goes to the heart of that law in which the Jew gloried (cf. vs. 23) and the transgressions selected are particularly well designed to expose the hypocrisy of the Jew and arouse him from the self-complacency into which his distorted conception of advantage had brought him (cf. Ps. 50:16–18).[3]

Stealing

How were the Jews, particularly those teaching the Law, breaking this, the eighth commandment? The accusations of Jesus against

2. James D. G. Dunn, as quoted by John Stott in *Romans: God's Good News for the World* (Downers Grove, Ill.: InterVarsity Press, 1994), p. 90.

3. John Murray, *The Epistle to the Romans* (Grand Rapids, Mich.: William B. Eerdmans Publishing Co., 1997), p. 83.

the religious leaders of His day give us some insight. He rebuked them for appearing righteous on the outside but being "full of robbery and self-indulgence" (Matt. 23:25). They had turned the temple into a profit-making enterprise (Mark 11:17). And Jesus called them thieves and robbers for leading the people, God's sheep, away from the true Shepherd (John 10:1–10).

Adultery

And what about adultery? Jesus clearly pointed out that adultery wasn't limited to just carrying out the act. Lust in the heart constituted adultery as well (Matt. 5:27–28). The scribes and Pharisees, whose unrighteousness Jesus clearly had in mind when He was teaching on this subject (v. 20), would have been guilty of this sin—right along with everyone else.

Idolatry

Can Paul rightly accuse the Jews of idolatry? Though they did bow down to idols under the wicked kings of Israel and Judah, idolatry as an organized practice for the Jews was nonexistent in New Testament times. The Jews' abhorrence of pagan idols was one of the characteristics of their religious system.

To find Paul's meaning, we need to look at his question, "Do you rob temples?" (Rom. 2:22b) more closely. Some have suggested that the Jews had made an idol out of money by hoarding for themselves funds meant for Jewish temple worship. Other commentators suggest that, though the Jews detested Gentile idol worship, they were not above making a profit from it. Some Jews may have been robbing pagan temples and selling the idols to other Gentile worshipers for a profit.[4] Or perhaps some Jews collected as art objects pagan idols seized and sold by Gentile armies. Whatever the case, their ill-gotten gain from pagan temples would itself have become an idol.

The bottom line for Paul was that the Jews were engaging in idolatry and other activities they condemned. They were breaking the very Law they were so proud of possessing, thus bringing dishonor to God (v. 23). Even the Gentiles noticed their failure to keep the Law:

> For "the name of God is blasphemed among the
> Gentiles because of you," just as it is written. (v. 24)

---

4. It's possible that this is the crime Paul and his companions were wrongly accused of in Acts 19:37.

Paul refers to Isaiah 52:5 here, which looks back to the Babylonian exile, where the captors of God's people made "sport of their God who was apparently unable to prevent [the Jews'] deportation (cf. Ezek 36:20, 21)."[5] Paul's application to the Jews in his day, commentator John Murray writes,

> is that the vices of the Jews give occasion to the Gentiles to blaspheme the name of God. The reasoning of the Gentiles is to the effect that a people are like their God and if the people can perpetrate such crimes their God must be of the same character and is to be execrated accordingly. The tragic irony is apparent. The Jews who claimed to be the leaders of the nations for the worship of the true God had become the instruments of provoking the nations to blasphemy. With this the indictment has reached its climax.[6]

Circumcision and Salvation

Picking up on the theme of the Law in light of Jew/Gentile relations, Paul moves to the topic of circumcision, a ceremonial rite the Jews treasured as a sign and guarantee of God's favor. They also believed that those who weren't circumcised—the Gentiles— were rejected by God. Further bolstering his argument that all humanity, Jews included, stand unrighteous and condemned before God, Paul denounces physical circumcision as insufficient for salvation.

> For indeed circumcision is of value if you practice the Law; but if you are a transgressor of the Law, your circumcision has become uncircumcision. So if the uncircumcised man keeps the requirements of the Law, will not his uncircumcision be regarded as circumcision? And he who is physically uncircumcised, if he keeps the Law, will he not judge you who though having the letter of the Law and circumcision are a transgressor of the Law? For he is not a Jew who is one outwardly, nor is circumcision that which

5. Everett F. Harrison, "Romans," in *The Expositor's Bible Commentary*, gen. ed. Frank E. Gaebelein (Grand Rapids, Mich.: Zondervan Publishing House, Regency Reference Library, 1976), vol. 10, p. 34.

6. Murray, *The Epistle to the Romans*, p. 85.

is outward in the flesh. But he is a Jew who is one inwardly; and circumcision is that which is of the heart, by the Spirit, not by the letter; and his praise is not from men, but from God. (Rom. 2:25–29)

Of What Value Is Circumcision?

Though circumcision was a sign of God's covenant relationship with Israel, it was a symbol of faith—faith that must be present for salvation. For example, Abraham was justified by faith *before* he was circumcised (see Gen. 15:6; 17:11; Gal. 3:6). And even though infants were to be circumcised on the eighth day, this was intended as a sign of future faith and obedience, not a guarantee of salvation.

For circumcision or any other rite to secure salvation, then, the whole of the Law must be obeyed along with it (Rom. 2:25; see also Gal. 3:10; James 2:10–11). And no one except Jesus Christ has ever been righteous enough to keep the Law.

Circumcision of the Heart

A person can be circumcised physically and be lost, or be uncircumcised physically and be saved (Rom. 2:26–27). It is circumcision of the heart—a new heart created by the Holy Spirit—that brings eternal life, not physical circumcision. And true salvation brings glory to God, not to human effort (vv. 28–29).

You can imagine how the Jews of Paul's day, who depended on human effort and ceremonial rites to gain favor with God, must have felt about Paul's dismantling their whole system of self-righteousness. Right standing before God apart from the Law? Apart from circumcision? Unthinkable!

What's really unthinkable, though, is trying to muster enough righteousness on our own to gain God's favor. Once Paul has settled that truth once and for all (the next chapter is our last one in the "sin section"), he'll shift from the problem of sin to the provision of the Savior. From hopelessness to hope. From the bankruptcy of our self-righteousness to the bounty of Christ's perfect righteousness.

But let's not get too far ahead. Let's stop here and take this chapter's lessons to heart.

✝ *Living Insights*

Since this section of Romans focuses particularly on Jewish practices, it may seem as though we're picking on the Jews. But we Christians can be guilty of the same violations. Think, for a moment, about some of the practices and traditions that have become a fixed part of the evangelical landscape in America—the things that mark individuals and congregations as evangelical Christians:

- Defending the Bible as true

- Baptism and the Lord's Supper

- Scripture memorization

- Participation in high-profile evangelism rallies

- Political activism

- Tithing

- Lists of "dos and don'ts"

- Christian "lingo"

- Church building programs

- Altar calls in the worship service

Not all of these things, in and of themselves, are necessarily bad. Some of them, in fact, are vital to the life and ministry of the church. But can any of them save an individual? Can any of them take the place of faith in Christ's life, death, and resurrection? No, they can't.

Yet some churches, by how much they emphasize certain aspects of religious life and downplay others, imply that these practices are more important than faith in Christ. Like the Jews who elevated circumcision over the faith it represented, we elevate our "rituals" over true faith in Christ.

How about you? Are you depending on anything besides Christ Himself for your salvation? Are you counting on achievements, memberships, traditions, or relationships to make you right with God and get you to heaven? How about your church? Does it uphold or overshadow the clear message of salvation in Christ alone? Write down whatever comes to mind.

_____

_____

_____

_____

_____

_____

_____

_____

_____

_____

_____

_____

_____

_____

   If you have been trusting in something besides Jesus to make you right with God, you can trust Him right now. Paul even tells us how, later in Romans:

> If you confess with your mouth Jesus as Lord, and believe in your heart that God raised Him from the dead, you will be saved; for with the heart a person believes, resulting in righteousness, and with the mouth he confesses, resulting in salvation. (Rom. 10:9–10)

Faith in Christ. That and that alone saves both Gentile and Jew.

Chapter 7

ARE WE REALLY THAT BAD?

Romans 3:1–20

Think back for a moment to Paul's words at the end of chapter 2.

> For he is not a Jew who is one outwardly, nor is circumcision that which is outward in the flesh. But he is a Jew who is one inwardly; and circumcision is that which is of the heart, by the Spirit, not by the letter; and his praise is not from men, but from God. (Rom. 2:28–29)

Imagine the indignation Paul's Jewish readers would have felt upon reading those words. "What do you mean, I'm not a Jew! I'm circumcised, am I not? I'm a descendant of Abraham! What kind of gibberish are you speaking, Paul—calling a Jew a non-Jew and a non-Jew a Jew? And you, of all people, Paul! Do you completely disregard your Hebrew heritage? Have you now turned on your own people, and do you now consider our history as God's people insignificant?"

As an accomplished contender for the faith, Paul anticipates just such a response. To head off these probable accusations, the great apostle next sets forth that the Jews, though not righteous in and of themselves, are indeed a privileged people.

Paul Answers the Jews' Objections

Verses 1–8 of chapter 3 are structured around four objections that Paul anticipates will come from his exposure of the Jews' guilt before God in 2:17–29.

Objection #1: Paul's Teaching Undermines God's Covenant Relationship with the Jews

> Then what advantage has the Jew? Or what is the benefit of circumcision? (3:1)

Most Jews who caught wind of Paul's argument would accuse him of teaching that, since being a true Jew is a matter of the heart and not nationality or circumcision, then being a physically circumcised

Jew is of no account. "What a slam to Judaism!" they would say. "Abraham, after all, was a Jew. And through him God established a covenant with His people. And circumcision was a sign of that covenant." Let's consider Paul's response.

> Great in every respect. First of all,[1] that they were
> entrusted with the oracles of God. (3:2)

Though being born Jewish did not give the Jews right standing before God, their being God's covenant people did indeed give them certain "advantages." The first, says Paul, is that they were given the "oracles of God"—the Old Testament Scriptures. The Old Testament traces the story of Israel, God's covenant people. Recorded by Jewish authors moved by the Holy Spirit, it contains the inspired record of God's faithfulness to His people. It sets forth the Law, God's holy standard for living. It records the prophecies and poetry that reveal God's heart for the people of His choosing. And it foreshadows and foretells Jesus Christ, Himself a Jew and the One who saves, not only Jews who put their trust in Him, but anyone who believes.

What a privilege to be the recipients and guardians of such treasure. While the other nations were in darkness, the Jews had been given the light of life. They have every right to look back on their national history with a sense of pride and sentimentality. What other nation has been so blessed by God? But do these privileges make them somehow better than everyone else? Not at all.

> In fact, the privileges made the Jews even more
> responsible to live up to God's requirements.
> Paul himself was a Jew, and even though he be-
> came a dynamic Christian, he did not turn his back
> on his heritage. In fact, he realized that the prophets,
> the law, and God's plan all pointed to fulfillment in
> Jesus Christ. Therefore, he could confidently state
> that being a Jew and being circumcised did have
> meaning, but only as part of God's total plan. The
> Jews were *entrusted with* God's words, preserving them

---

1. Paul's "first of all" in 3:2 sets us up for a list of advantages possessed by the Jews. However, he doesn't resume the list until 9:4, after taking several chapters to expound the truth of justification by faith and the believer's new status in Christ.

until the coming of Christ, who was the fulfillment
of the prophetic Scriptures.[2]

So, God's covenant relationship with the nation of Israel and
the rite of circumcision have significance as part of redemptive
history. But these do not secure salvation. They only point to Christ,
the mediator of the new covenant (see Luke 22:20; Heb. 8:7–13)
and the One who circumcises our hearts through faith (Rom. 2:29).

Objection #2: Paul's Teaching Calls God's Faithfulness into Question

Paul and his critics agree: the Jews are a privileged people. Yet
it's no secret that not all Jews live according to His word or trust
in His promises. Does their faithlessness impact God's faithfulness?
Does it mean that the Jews are not His covenant people after all?

Paul will develop the place of the Jews in God's redemptive
plan in Romans 9–11. For now, though, he reminds the Jews from
their own Scriptures that the sinful actions of humans do not nullify
the faithfulness of God.

> What then? If some did not believe, their unbelief
> will not nullify the faithfulness of God, will it? May
> it never be! Rather, let God be found true, though
> every man be found a liar, as it is written,
> "That you may be justified in Your words,
> And prevail when You are judged."[3]
> (Rom. 3:3–4)

In a dialogue format between Paul and his figurative objector,
commentator William Barclay helps make the connection between
verses 1–2 and verses 3–4 clear.

> *The objector:* What, then, is the difference [be-
> tween Jew and Gentile]?

---

2. Bruce B. Barton, David R. Veerman, and Neil Wilson, *Romans,* Life Application Bible
Commentary Series (Wheaton, Ill.: Tyndale House Publishers, 1992), p. 62.

3. Here Paul quotes Psalm 51:4 from the Septuagint, the Greek version of the Old Testament.
In that psalm, David is confessing his sin of adultery with Bathsheba. In doing so, he
acknowledges that his sin in no way damages the character of God. David is responsible for
his own actions. Perhaps another reason Paul chose to use David as an example of God's
faithfulness in light of humanity's unfaithfulness, is that God promised He would raise up a
king from David's line who would rule forever (2 Sam. 7:16). And not even David's sin nullified
that promise. Jesus, the promised King, was indeed a descendant of David (Matt. 1:1–17).

Paul: For one thing, the Jew possesses what the Gentile never so directly possessed—the commandments of God.

The objector: Granted! But what if some of the Jews disobeyed these commandments and were unfaithful to God and came under his condemnation? You have just said that God gave the Jews a special position and a special promise. Now you go on to say that at least some of them are under the condemnation of God. Does that mean that God has broken his promise and shown himself to be unjust and unreliable?

Paul: Far from it! What it does show is that there is no favoritism with God and that he punishes sin wherever he sees it. The very fact that he condemns the unfaithful Jews is the best possible proof of his absolute justice. He might have been expected to overlook the sins of this special people of his but he does not.[4]

It is precisely God's faithfulness—to His word, His holiness, His justice—in light of our unfaithfulness that makes Him trustworthy. Even the most conscientious and dependable people will let us down at one time or another. But God is forever faithful. That means our salvation in Christ is secure. It means He never leaves us, even during our darkest hours. And it means that our place in heaven is assured. We belong to Him. And He'll be waiting to welcome us when this life is over . . . just like He said.

Objection #3: Paul's Teaching Presents a Twisted View of God's Justice

If God's faithfulness is upheld in spite of our unfaithfulness, then it follows that His righteousness is upheld in spite of our unrighteousness. But Paul's objectors would argue that this isn't fair of God, as Paul reflects in his next two questions.

> But if our unrighteousness demonstrates the righteousness of God, what shall we say? The God who inflicts

4. William Barclay, *The Letter to the Romans,* rev. ed., The Daily Study Bible Series (Philadelphia, Pa.: Westminster Press, 1975), pp. 51–52.

wrath is not unrighteous, is He? (I am speaking in human terms.) (v. 5)

Here's the gist of the objector's argument:

> *And if my sinfulness makes God look so good, then why should he punish me?* I'm actually helping him out! This was an attempt to make it seem unjust for God to punish sinners.[5]

Paul's answer to this objection?

> May it never be![6] For otherwise, how will God judge the world? (v. 6)

Would the Jews' same argument of sin highlighting God's righteousness hold true for the rest of the world? No—they looked forward to God's judgment of the nations' sins. So Paul has exposed the absurd double standard of this objection. But he doesn't stop there.

Objection # 4: Paul's Teaching Promotes Sinful Living as the Path to God's Glory

Continuing with the objectors' idea of our sinfulness somehow making God look good, Paul asks,

> But if through my lie the truth of God abounded to His glory, why am I also still being judged as a sinner? And why not say (as we are slanderously reported and as some claim that we say), "Let us do evil that good may come"? Their condemnation is just. (vv. 7–8)

"Why in the world is God judging us for sinning when our sinning actually glorifies Him? Shouldn't we sin all the more, and so glorify Him all the more? And isn't that what Paul is teaching anyway? Doesn't his grace-oriented message cause us to abandon morally responsible living?" That's the essence of the dissenters' complaint.

Paul simply responds, "Their condemnation is just" (v. 8). Anyone who so impugns God's ways or distorts the gospel is deserving of judgment.

---

5. Barton, Veerman, and Wilson, *Romans*, p. 64.

6. "May it never be!" is Paul's emphatic response to a false conclusion drawn from a true statement. Compare a similar use of this phrase in Romans 6:1–2.

So, to summarize Paul's argument in 3:1–8, the Jews are a privileged people because God entered into a covenant relationship with them. But the rejection of Him by a great number of Jews does not nullify God's promises to them. Furthermore, the sinfulness of humanity neither diminishes the perfect character of God nor renders His gospel ineffective.

Having shown Judaism to be valuable, God to be just, and the gospel to be valid, Paul now turns his attention once again to the universal depravity of all humanity.

The Final Verdict

Are the Jews a special people, blessed by God? Yes, Paul has said. Does that privileged status guarantee the salvation of all who are of Hebrew descent? Absolutely not. Both Jews and Gentiles stand as sinners before our holy God.

> What then? Are we [Jews] better than they [Gentiles]? Not at all; for we have already charged that both Jews and Greeks are all under sin. (v. 9)

From the declaration of universal sinfulness, Paul now moves to a graphic description of it. In verses 10–18, he lifts the lid off the trash bin of human depravity and bids us look inside. So hold your breath and . . .

> as it is written,
> "There is none righteous, not even one;
> There is none who understands,
> There is none who seeks for God;
> All have turned aside, together they have
> become useless;
> There is none who does good,
> There is not even one."
> "Their throat is an open grave,
> With their tongues they keep deceiving,"
> "The poison of asps is under their lips";
> "Whose mouth is full of cursing and bitterness";
> "Their feet are swift to shed blood,
> Destruction and misery are in their paths,
> And the path of peace they have not known."
> "There is no fear of God before their eyes."

Whew, that's gross! Can Paul really be talking about all humanity here? Sounds like he's describing the worst of the worst—characters from a horror movie or criminals from the FBI's "most wanted" list. How can such a description do justice to the whole human race? Dividing this passage into two sections will help us understand Paul's words.

Sin Separates the Whole Human Race from God (vv. 10–12)

Paul draws upon several Old Testament passages, beginning with Psalms 14:1–3 and 53:1–3, to drive home the point that he has been making all along: absolutely no one is righteous apart from Christ. We are all sinners. In our natural, sinful state, we can't truly understand the things of God. We can't pursue a relationship with Him. In fact, we deliberately turn away from Him and turn to our own interests. None of us "does good."

This doesn't mean that the unsaved can't perform acts of virtue. Many unsaved people give of their time, resources, and talents to help the poor, promote the arts, strengthen the family, even build churches. By "good," however, Paul isn't talking about positive contributions to society. He's talking about good as God defines good—conforming to His will out of a heart that loves Him. And that is only possible by believing in Jesus Christ. Only He can forgive our sins and move us from self-orientation to God-orientation.

Sin Permeates the Whole Person (vv. 13–18)

In the next six verses, Paul segues from the universal scope of sin to its personal impact. Drawing again upon several Old Testament passages—Psalm 5:9; 10:7; 36:1; 140:3; Isaiah 59:7—he shows that no part of our person is unaffected by sin. Notice how much emphasis Paul places on our speech ("throat," "tongues," "lips," "mouth"). Jesus said, "The things that proceed out of the mouth come from the heart, and those defile the man" (Matt. 15:18). So our speech—lying, cursing, gossip, idle talk—reveals the sin that resides in our hearts.

Sin also manifests itself in our actions. It causes people to murder, destroy the lives of others, live without peace, and reject God instead of fear Him. Our intellect, speech, will, and actions are all corrupted by sin.

This is what theologians through the ages have referred to as the doctrine of "total depravity." Often misunderstood, total depravity doesn't mean that we're all as bad as we can possibly be.

Not everyone, for example, stoops as low as Hitler or Nero.

What total depravity *does* mean is that we're sinful through and through. It's an issue of extent more than it is degree. Even the most helpful, generous, clean-living person is shot through with sin. That's our nature; that's how we're born (see Ps. 51:5). Total depravity means that we're utterly incapable of taking one step toward God without His miraculous grace.

Imagine a gallon jug of pure drinking water. Now take an eyedropper and add a few drops of raw sewage. Shake the jug vigorously. Would you drink the water now? No way! Even if the water still looks pure, even if it's not as dirty as it could be, it's still infected throughout with sewage. There's no part of that water that hasn't been tainted. And there's no way it can become pure again without undergoing some kind of purification process.

That's a picture of total depravity. We are born impure, permeated with sin. And we're as helpless to purify ourselves as that jug of water is to purify itself. Purification must come from the outside. We must be granted, as John Calvin said, a foreign righteousness. A righteousness from God Himself. The righteousness that comes through faith in Christ Jesus.

Sin Comes to Light by the Law

Just in case some of Paul's readers, namely the Jews, might have missed the point and read verses 10–18 as applying only to the Gentiles—those without the Law—Paul closes this sin section with a final word about sin and the Law.

> Now we know that whatever the Law says, it speaks to those who are under the Law, so that every mouth may be closed and all the world may become accountable to God; because by the works of the Law no flesh will be justified in His sight; for through the Law comes the knowledge of sin. (Rom. 3:19–20)

The Law, then—whether codified for the Jews or embedded in the conscience of the Gentiles—cannot justify us before God. It cannot make us righteous. It can only show us our sin, so that we stand silent and guilty before our Judge. Powerless to change. Awaiting His sentence.

This case, however, is not closed! As Paul tells us in the next chapter, our Judge is also our Savior. He who condemns also sets free. He who shows us our sin through the Law removes our sin through Christ and allows us to trade in our prison clothes for a shining robe of righteousness. Freedom, mercy, grace . . . daylight. They're just around the corner.

✝ *Living Insights*

Congratulations! You've made it through one of the toughest sections of Scripture. Romans 1:18–3:20 is no picnic. It's an exposé of our sinfulness—a wincing, breath-holding analysis of the underbelly of humanity.

This trek through the sewer of depravity, though uncomfortable, is necessary. How are we to understand salvation unless we understand what we have been saved from or how utterly unable we are to save ourselves? How can we ask for mercy if we don't believe we deserve judgment? How will we be thankful for the work of Christ if we think we can work our way to God? And how amazed will we be by God's grace if we're not appalled by our sin?

Before going on, why not take a moment to outline the major truths you've learned in 1:18–3:20.

_____

_____

_____

_____

_____

_____

_____

_____

_____

_____

_____

See you at dawn.

Chapter 8

THE *ONLY* WAY TO GOD
Romans 3:21–31

A few words can change your whole life for the better. Turn sadness into joy. Desperation into hope. Darkness into light. For example:

"The tumor is benign."

"We found your little girl; she's safe."

"The surgery was a success."

"The tornado didn't touch down."

"The war is over!"

"I forgive you."

Amazing, isn't it—the healing power of words? Yet it's not the words alone that heal. It's how and when they're delivered. Tone and timing make all the difference. Words we spray about haphazardly a hundred times a day, when applied in the right context, become more than words. They become blankets against the chilling wind of uncertainty. A strong hand to pull us out of the quagmire of doubt and despair. Bridges from death to life.

And so it is with Paul's first two words in Romans 3:21: "But now." They are a light at the end of the sin-tunnel we've been slogging through since 1:18. So let's not waste another moment. Let's run to receive the good news he has for us.

God Provides What He Requires: His Own Righteousness

> But now apart from the Law the righteousness
> of God has been manifested, being witnessed by the
> Law and the Prophets. (3:21)

Apart from the Law, Foretold in the Law

As we step from the darkness into light, Paul takes us from our inability to God's ability. Two important points stand out in this single verse. First, God has made known a righteousness that is apart from the Law. That is, it has nothing to do with our having to keep the Law—since, as Paul has already made clear earlier, no one is capable of keeping the Law.

And second, this righteousness that comes apart from the Law is not a new invention. It was witnessed by the "Law and the Prophets"; it appears throughout the entire Old Testament. The writers of the Old Testament, though they didn't possess the fully revealed gospel as we have it today, nonetheless knew and taught that a person was justified by faith apart from the Law. Paul later cites Abraham and David as examples of Old Testament believers who received God's righteousness by faith (4:1–8). Add to these the sacrificial system with its blood sacrifices, the duties of priests, the reign of kings, and countless other images and prefigurings of Christ, and there's no missing the gospel's presence in the Old Testament.

In Paul's day, however, that gospel wasn't just embedded in the Old Testament. It was now "manifested"—clearly displayed through the life and death of Christ and the writings of Paul and other apostles.

Available through Faith in Christ

Righteousness being manifested, though, isn't sufficient for salvation. This righteousness from God must be embraced by faith.

> Even the righteousness of God through faith in Jesus Christ for all those who believe; for there is no distinction; for all have sinned and fall short of the glory of God. (vv. 22–23)

All have sinned; no one is righteous. Paul established that in 1:18–3:20. He states that truth again here, not so much to return to the topic of universal sinfulness but to encourage us that the gospel, like sin, isn't confined to any particular race of people. "All those" who believe in Christ—whether Jew or Gentile, male or female, slave or free—will be granted His righteousness (see also Gal. 3:28).

A Gift to Us, a Payment to God

That means God's righteousness is a gift; we can't earn it.

> Being justified as a gift by His grace through the redemption which is in Christ Jesus. (v. 24)

A wage is something you earn, something you work for. God's grace, however, is His gift to us—exactly the opposite of what we deserve. And it comes to us only one way—through the blood of Jesus Christ.

Paul says we're "justified" as a gift (v. 24). That means God declares us righteous while we are still sinners. *Justification* is a legal declaration, an announcement of one's status before God. Its opposite is condemnation. Justification doesn't mean that we become instantly perfect and holy. But we are instantly forgiven and loved by God. Christ's righteousness is instantly credited to our account. So when God looks at us, He sees the perfect obedience and holiness of His Son. Once justified, the process of spiritual growth—*sanctification*—begins.

Redemption is a term used in the slave trade. It pictures our being purchased and delivered from the ownership of Satan and sin by Christ's blood and made free in Him.

Though justification is a gift to us, it cost God a great deal. It cost Him the life of His Son. In His crucifixion, Jesus was

> displayed publicly as a propitiation in His blood through faith. This was to demonstrate His righteousness, because in the forbearance of God He passed over the sins previously committed; for the demonstration, I say, of His righteousness at the present time, so that He would be just and the justifier of the one who has faith in Jesus. (vv. 25–26)

Propitiation is a fancy theological word that means "satisfaction." Jesus' death was necessary to satisfy God's need to judge sin—the sins of all those who would believe in Him.

This is important, because it preserves God as the just judge of sin, even though we have been forgiven. If He had simply overlooked our sins and not judged them, He would not have been a just judge. After all, God even instructed His people in the Old Testament to punish wickedness and reward righteousness (Deut. 32:41; Ps. 9:7–8; 62:12). Was He not willing to do as much?

That's the wonder of the Cross. By pouring out His wrath on His own Son, God rightly judged our sin—even those sins "previously committed": past sins that deserved His judgment but were judged in Christ on the Cross. That's only half the story, though. Not only was our sinfulness transferred to Christ and paid for by His blood, His perfect righteousness was transferred to our account. Thus God retains His character as a just judge of sin while extending mercy to us in Christ.

No Room for Boasting

What, then, should our response be to God's giving us such a gracious gift? "Wow! Look at the gift I earned." "Boy, did I ever deserve that!" Not hardly. The gift of salvation glorifies the Giver, not the recipient. There is no room for boasting.

> Where then is boating? It is excluded. By what kind of law? Of works? No, but by a law of faith. For we maintain that a man is justified by faith apart from works of the Law. (Rom. 3:27–28)

Not by the Law

Commentator Leon Morris explains why there's no room for spiritual pride in the Christian life.

> If the cross has done all that is needed . . . if God has revealed in the Old Testament that human effort is futile . . . there is no place for man's effort and accordingly for man's extolling of his own effort. In any religion of law the worshipper may legitimately feel satisfaction in his personal achievement, but this is a satisfaction that can lead to pride. For those saved by grace, however, that is impossible. Grace leaves no place for satisfaction in one's own achieve- ment, for salvation is all of God. . . . Some such pride is the besetting sin of all religious people, no matter what their religion. But as the hymn writer puts it, "When I survey the wondrous cross . . . I pour contempt on all my pride." To understand what grace and faith mean is to reject the way of pride and boasting.[1]

By the phrase "law of faith," Paul means a system of faith as opposed to a system of works. If a person is to be justified before God, it is faith in Christ that serves as the linchpin of the system. For a person is justified "by faith apart from works of the Law" (v. 28).

For Jews and Gentiles

To further emphasize the futility of pride, Paul reminds his

---

1. Leon Morris, *The Epistle to the Romans* (1988; reprint, Grand Rapids, Mich.: William B. Eerdmans Publishing Co., 1992), p. 185.

readers to beware of national pride—thinking that God's grace is bestowed only on the Jews.

> Or is God the God of Jews only? Is He not the God of Gentiles also? Yes, of Gentiles also, since indeed God who will justify the circumcised by faith and the uncircumcised through faith is one. (vv. 29–30)

God's graciousness extends to all people, all nations. He welcomes all into His kingdom who trust His Son by faith.

What about the Law?

Since Paul argues so forcefully in Romans that justification comes by faith in Christ and not by keeping the Law, he must periodically remind his readers that he's not saying the Law is evil or even that believers should ignore it. That's what he does here when he says:

> Do we then nullify the Law through faith? May it never be! On the contrary, we establish the Law. (v. 31)

Justification by faith upholds the value of the Law in two ways. First, it shows the true purpose of the Law, which was to reveal our sinfulness and drive us to Christ. Second, through justification by faith we actually keep the Law when we walk in the Spirit (see Rom. 8:3–4). As believers clothed in Christ's righteousness and indwelled by His Holy Spirit, our works are no longer empty. They grow out of a heart for God, and they please Him.

True righteousness. Given to us as a gift. Ours by faith, apart from the Law. All because of Christ. That's the flip side of sin. The light in the darkness. The hope that comes with the morning. Seize the day!

Living Insights

After all this discussion of justification by faith alone, I'm going to throw you a curve: It's also true to say that salvation is by works. No, I haven't suddenly embraced the communication tactics of political spin doctors—trying to pass off falsehood as truth. But "salvation is by faith" and "salvation is by works" are both true statements. How can that be?

The answer lies in how we answer the question, "*Whose* faith and *whose* works?" As Paul has argued so passionately, *our* works cannot save us. None of us can live a good enough life to earn God's favor—because none of us can keep the Law. We can only be saved by faith. In whom, though, is that faith?

It's in Jesus Christ, who *did* live a perfectly obedient life under the Law. He *earned* salvation for us. We are saved by placing *our* faith in *His* works. See how it happens?

Jesus' earning eternal life for us by keeping the Law is often called His "active obedience." This is just as important as His "passive obedience," His death on the Cross. Yet we often focus so much on Jesus' death that we forget He lived a perfect life. If He had disobeyed even one of God's commandments, He would have been a lawbreaker, and He would have disqualified Himself as the One who could earn eternal life for us. For thirty-three years, Jesus kept the Law without fail. That perfect obedience is transferred to our account when we believe in Him. The words of theologian Loraine Boettner remind us why Christ's passive and active obedience are both crucial to our understanding of salvation.

> By that life of spotless perfection, then, Jesus acquired for His people a positive righteousness which is imputed to them and which secures for them life in heaven. All that Christ has done and suffered is regarded as having been done and suffered by them. In Him they have fulfilled the law of perfect obedience, as also in Him they have borne the penalty for their sins. By His passive obedience they have been rescued from hell; and by His active obedience they are given entrance into heaven.[2]

So, our salvation is more than just a rescue—it's a reward. We're like death row inmates set free after someone else agreed to die in our place. But upon release, we're given a new home to live in and unlimited financial resources. Rescue and reward. Neither of which we deserve. Both of which come to us because of Christ's loving obedience to the Father . . . and His love for us.

No wonder they call it amazing grace.

---

2. Loraine Boettner, *Studies in Theology* (Phillipsburg, N.J.: Presbyterian and Reformed Publishing Co., 1947), pp. 300–1.

Chapter 9

FAITH: GOD'S PLAN
FROM THE START
Romans 4:1–13

For sixty-four verses, we strained our eyes peering into the darkness of unregenerate souls and the futility of working our way into a right standing with God (1:18–3:20). We stumbled over degradation and depravity, heartlessness and hypocrisy. Things we don't like to look at, let alone confess.

But then, in 3:21–31, Paul finally led us into the light of God's grace. What a joyous relief! We learned that we're not trapped in the oppressive gloom of our own sins, because God Himself has reached out to us with redemption and the gift of His own righteousness. A righteousness that we receive by faith.

Faith. It is so simple, so humble, so rooted in gratitude. And it so goes against our nature. Paul knew it. He understood more than most how much we like to establish our own rightness and earn our own way (see his litany of good deeds in Phil. 3:4–6). And that's why, in Romans 4, he gives us a lesson in the primacy of faith. For before the Law of Moses, before the seal of circumcision, was God's covenant of faith with Abraham.

Faith is not new to salvation, Paul contends; it was God's redemptive plan from the very start. Let's join the apostle as he illuminates these truths with Abraham's story.

Beginning at the Beginning

Paul builds his case for faith with the father of the faith, Abraham, the one God promised would be the progenitor of blessing for all the nations (Gen. 12:3). And he starts with this question,

> What then shall we say that Abraham, our fore-
> father according to the flesh, has found? (Rom. 4:1)

What did Abraham know about righteousness through faith in God versus justification based on his own righteous works? After all, he was a righteous man, the friend of God. Jewish tradition even asserted that "Abraham had been chosen by God for his unique role in history because he was the only righteous man alive at the time."[1] He was the Jews' premier example of righteousness through works (Gen. 26:3–5). But Paul discovered something else.

Even Abraham Cannot Boast

"If," Paul begins, "Abraham was justified by works, he has something to boast about" (v. 2a). For an ordinary human being to live a life of perfect righteousness so that he or she would be acceptable to God would be quite a feat to brag of! However, we know that Abraham was not perfect; his human sins include twice lying about Sarah not being his wife (Gen. 12:10–20; chap. 20). So much for a perfect record. Which is why Paul finishes his thought: "but not before God" (Rom. 4:2b).

God is perfect; He is holy. Righteousness has its origin in Him; we only know good because of Him. How, then, can a finite, fallible, and frail human being possibly stand and boast of one's goodness in God's awesome presence? Even at our best, we are riddled with flaws, and the very act of boasting would reveal the sin of pride! If we have to depend on ourselves, we are without hope.

Only God Can Provide Justification

Paul, however, sets us straight with Scripture's infallible record:

> For what does Scripture say? "Abraham believed
> God, and it was credited to him as righteousness."
> (v. 3)

Abraham trusted in God's goodness, believed He would keep His word to him, and built his life on it. Notice, he didn't just acknowledge that God exists—his belief was much more specific than that. God had promised him,

> "Do not fear, Abram,
> I am a shield to you;
> Your reward shall be very great. . . .
> One who will come forth from your own body, he shall
> be your heir." And He took him outside and said,
> "Now look toward the heavens, and count the stars,
> if you are able to count them." And He said to him,
> "So shall your descendants be." (Gen. 15:1, 4b–5)

---

1. Bruce B. Barton, David R. Veerman, and Neil Wilson, *Romans*, Life Application Bible Commentary Series (Wheaton, Ill.: Tyndale House Publishers, 1992), p. 81.

And Abraham "believed in the Lord; and He reckoned it to him as righteousness" (v. 6). He did not work for his right standing with God or earn it as if it were his rightful wage—as if God were obligated by contract to pay him (Rom. 4:4). No, Abraham took his place with the rest of us "ungodly" people,[2] and God "credited" his faith as righteousness (v. 5).

To further amplify his point, Paul turns to the man after God's own heart, Israel's greatest king and recipient of another covenant and messianic promise from God, David.

> Just as David also speaks of the blessing on the man to whom God credits righteousness apart from works:
> "Blessed are those whose lawless deeds have been forgiven,
> And whose sins have been covered.
> Blessed is the man whose sin the Lord will not take into account." (vv. 6–8)

The greatest happiness, David exults in this quote from Psalm 32, belongs to those whose sins God has sent away, covered over with atonement, whose slate He has wiped clean.[3] Once God has forgiven us, He never brings up that sin again. When the late Corrie ten Boom returned to Germany, the land where she suffered in a concentration camp and where her sister died, she brought this great message of God's forgiveness to those "bitter, bombed-out" people.

> "When we confess our sins," I said, "God casts them into the deepest ocean, gone forever. And even though I cannot find a Scripture for it, I believe God then places a sign out there that says, NO FISHING ALLOWED."[4]

It All Comes on "Credit"

Four times now Paul has used the word *credited* or *credits* (he'll

---

2. Joshua 24:2 tells us that Abraham's father, Terah, "served other gods." It is possible that Abraham, having been raised in that environment, was an idolater too. God took Abraham out of that pagan darkness and brought him "into His marvelous light" (1 Pet. 2:9).

3. See James Montgomery Boice, *Romans, Volume 1: Justification by Faith (Romans 1–4)* (Grand Rapids, Mich.: Baker Book House, 1991), pp. 449–51.

4. Corrie ten Boom, with Jamie Buckingham, *Tramp for the Lord* (Fort Washington, Pa.: Christian Literature Crusade; Old Tappan, N.J.: Fleming H. Revell Co., 1974), p. 55.

use it ten times in all in Romans 4). What exactly does this idea of "credit" mean? Why would God honor our faith by giving us righteousness? What do David's sins not being taken into account have to do with righteousness being credited to Abraham's account?

First of all, as John Stott explains, it helps us to understand that the verb *credits* or *credited* (*logizomai* in Greek) is often

> used in a financial or commercial context, it signifies to put something to somebody's account, as when Paul wrote to Philemon about Onesimus: "If he has done you any wrong or owes you anything, charge it to me."[5] (see Philem. 18)

In bringing together Abraham's and David's examples, Paul is showing that

> justification involves a double counting, crediting, or reckoning. On the one hand, negatively, God will never count our sins against us. On the other hand, positively, God credits our account with righteousness, as a free gift, by faith, altogether apart from our works.[6]

How can God do this? Through Christ, who lived a perfectly righteous life under the Law, who paid the price for our sins with His death, taking them away and nailing them to the cross, and who raised us to a new, righteous life through His resurrection and triumph over death. In short, by God's grace and mercy alone, we got what we did not deserve—righteousness; and we didn't get what we did deserve—punishment for our sins.

Christ's work covers Old Testament believers too, or else Paul would not have used their examples in his argument. They looked ahead to God's promise of a Deliverer who would come (see Gen. 3:15; John 8:56; Gal. 3:6–9; Heb. 11:10), just as we look back to the promise of the Deliverer who has already come.[7]

---

5. John Stott, *Romans: God's Good News for the World* (Downers Grove, Ill.: InterVarsity Press, 1994), p. 125.

6. Stott, *Romans*, p. 127.

7. For an excellent study of this passage and the issue of how believers in the Old Testament were saved before Christ's actual coming, we highly recommend that you consult James Montgomery Boice, *Romans, Volume 1: Justification by Faith (Romans 1–4)* (Grand Rapids, Mich.: Baker Book House, 1991), chaps. 51–53, pp. 429–52.

What about the Covenant of Circumcision?

Paul's Jewish audience may have been thrown for a loop by what Paul was showing them from Scripture. Surely, they would insist, God's gift of justification, His blessing of righteousness, applies only to those who obeyed the covenant of circumcision as Abraham did. But Paul challenges their thinking with an irrefutable argument.

Righteousness through Circumcision?

> Is this blessedness only for the circumcised, or also for the uncircumcised? We have been saying that Abraham's faith was credited to him as righteousness. Under what circumstances was it credited? Was it after he was circumcised, or before? It was not after, but before! (Rom. 4:9–10 NIV)

Again rooting his logic in Scripture, Paul reminds his readers that at least thirteen years passed between Abraham's faith being credited to him as righteousness (Gen. 15:6) and God instituting the covenant of circumcision (chap. 17). How do we know this? Because following God's promises in Genesis 15, Abraham fathered Ishmael through Sarah's handmaid, Hagar (chap. 16). When Ishmael was born, Abraham was eighty-six years old (16:16), and when Abraham obeyed God's command to be circumcised, he was ninety-nine years old (17:24).

Righteousness Only through Faith!

Paul's point is that Abraham's righteousness did not come from obeying God and being circumcised; rather, circumcision was only a seal of the righteousness that was *already* his (Rom. 4:11a). This is a crucial point in Paul's argument, because if Abraham was uncircumcised when he was declared righteous, then he is really not just the father of the Jews but

> the father of all who believe without being circumcised, that righteousness might be credited to them. (v. 11b)

Who are the uncircumcised? The Gentiles! Paul has proved from the Jews' own Scriptures that the doors of God's salvation have been thrown wide open to anyone and everyone—regardless of race, color, nationality, or background—who comes to God by faith.

Now, this offer certainly does not exclude the Jews, the circumcised. Instead, it shows that both Jews and Gentiles come to God the same way: through faith in Jesus Christ alone. As Paul says, Abraham is also

> the father of circumcision to those who not only are of the circumcision, but *who also follow in the steps of the faith of our father Abraham* which he had while uncircumcised. (v. 12, emphasis added)

Not even the Law of Moses, which came centuries after God credited Abraham with righteousness, supersedes the way of faith.

> For the promise to Abraham or to his descendants that he would be heir of the world was not through the Law, but through the righteousness of faith. (v. 13, see also Gal. 3:17–18)

It all starts with faith. And it has always started with faith. Faith has been God's plan from the very beginning. And it will be His plan to the very end.

In whom is your faith placed? In yourself and your good works? In your ability to lead a "good enough" life? Or is your faith placed in God—placed in His provision of Jesus Christ, who lived the *only* life that was and will ever be good enough for a perfect and holy God? He alone can wipe your slate clean and give you His own unlimited righteousness. Abraham counted on it and was richly blessed. Let's follow in his proven footsteps.

✝ *Living Insights*

Eugene Peterson, in *The Message*, renders Romans 4:2–5 this way:

> If Abraham, by what he *did* for God, got God to approve him, he could certainly have taken credit for it. But the story we're given is a God-story, not an Abraham-story. What we read in Scripture is, "Abraham entered into what God was doing for him, and *that* was the turning point. He trusted God to set him right instead of trying to be right on his own."
>
> If you're a hard worker and do a good job, you deserve your pay; we don't call your wages a gift. But

if you see that the job is too big for you, that it's something only *God* can do, and you trust him to do it—you could never do it for yourself no matter how hard and long you worked—well, that trusting-him-to-do-it is what gets you set right with God, *by* God. Sheer gift.[8]

How does the story of your faith read? Is it a God-story, or is it a you-story? What do you think Peterson means by that? How does the idea of "crediting" relate to this?

_____

_____

_____

_____

_____

God wants to clear our spiritual ledgers of all our sins, marking them PAID BY CHRIST, and He wants to transfer Christ's perfect righteousness to our accounts. That sounds almost too good to be true, doesn't it? Do you believe it? Do you struggle with it in any way? How is it hard to accept, either for you or others you've talked with? Why are our own works so hard to give up?

_____

_____

_____

_____

Can you fathom the love behind God's offer, His "sheer gift"? He has no reason to save and justify us—other than love. Great, unconditional, vast, providing love. Spend some time thinking about this God "who justifies the ungodly"—you and me (v. 5). Meditate on His justice and His grace, which come together so

8. Eugene H. Peterson, *The Message: The New Testament in Contemporary English* (Colorado Springs, Colo.: NavPress, 1993), p. 310.

perfectly in His Son, Jesus Christ. Then thank Him, give Him the credit for crediting you with everything you need for eternal life.

_____

_____

_____

_____

_____

_____

_____

_____

_____

_____

_____

_____

_____

_____

_____

_____

_____

_____

_____

_____

_____

Chapter 10

THE MAN WHO HOPED AGAINST HOPE
Romans 4:13–25

As we continue to learn from the faith of Abraham, we need to be careful. Careful? Of what? Of thinking that faith came easily for Abraham. Of believing that faith should come easily for us.

It is true that faith is trusting that God will bring about what we don't yet see (Heb. 11:1). But faith is not putting on rose-colored glasses; it's not a "great attitude" that denies the pain and struggle of waiting. Faith often has to wrestle and cling and hold on for dear life—it has to persist and endure.

> Great faith is not the faith that walks always in the light and knows no darkness, but the faith that perseveres in spite of God's seeming silences, and that faith will most certainly and surely get its reward.[1]

Abraham would attest to that. His given name, Abram, meant "Exalted Father," yet he was childless for most of his life, due to his wife Sarai's inability to conceive. In that ancient culture, barrenness was a disgrace to the whole family. How painful to have everyone else call him "Exalted Father," yet never to hear those words from a child of his own! God, though, had plans for him.

When Abram was seventy-five, God called him to leave his home and go to a new land, where He promised to "make [him] a great nation" and bless "all the families of the earth" through him (Gen. 12:2–3).

Surely now the child would come! But ten years passed. No child. No nation. God came to him again and reiterated His promise, even more specifically: "One who will come forth from your own body, he shall be your heir. . . . Now look toward the heavens, and count the stars, if you are able to count them. . . . So shall your descendants be" (15:4–5). Confident that God would do as He said but not clear on how He would do it, Abram and Sarai used Hagar, Sarai's maid, as a surrogate mother. Ishmael was born

---

1. *The Harper Religious and Inspirational Quotation Companion*, comp. and ed. Margaret Pepper (New York, N.Y.: Harper and Row, Publishers, 1989), p. 172.

when Abram was eighty-six (chap. 16). But the child of Hagar was not the child of God's covenant.

Thirteen years passed before Abram heard from the Lord again. When he did, God changed his name to Abraham, "Father of a Multitude," reconfirming His promise that Abraham would have an heir through Sarai, renamed Sarah ("Princess"), who would be the mother of nations. This time, God cleared the way for what had been His plan all along. Isaac was born the following year—twenty-five years after God's first promise.

Twenty-five years!

No, faith is not a pleasure ride. It demands patience and perseverance. It sometimes entails sacrifice—of the way we dreamed things would be, of surrogate solutions that weren't part of God's plan. Most of all, faith requires vulnerability . . . trusting a God we can't control, relying on a timetable not of our making. But believing that, no matter what, He is good and He keeps His word.

The Promise versus the Law

Of course, faith—dependence on God's character and faithfulness—has been Paul's topic for some time now. He has shown us that by Abraham's faith, not by his good works or his ritual of circumcision, he was credited with righteousness by God (Rom. 4:1–12). Paul now explains that Abraham's faith in God's promise also takes priority over the Mosaic Law.

> For the promise to Abraham or to his descendants that he would be heir of the world[2] was not through the Law, but through the righteousness of faith. For if those who are of the Law are heirs, faith is made void and the promise is nullified; for the Law brings about wrath, but where there is no law, there also is no violation. (vv. 13–15)

God made His promise to Abraham *four centuries* before He gave His holy Law to Moses. So the promised blessings did not depend on Abraham's performance; they sprang from God and His

2. In His unconditional generosity, the Lord bestowed on Abraham his key part in salvation history: through him and his descendants, the Messiah, Jesus Christ, would come. This is why Paul said Abraham and his progeny would be "heir of the world." Christ is the true ruler of the world, so those who have become God's children through Christ's reconciling work will possess all the earth as an inheritance from Him (see Matt. 5:5; 1 Cor. 3:21–23; Eph. 1:3–12).

generosity. God's promise was unconditional, one-sided—not a contract imposing conditions that Abraham had to keep in order to receive due blessings from God. If the promise was altered by conditions, then it would no longer be an unconditional promise. It would be "nullified," and faith would be "made void" because Abraham wouldn't have been trusting in God but in his own ability to earn a right standing with God.

Paul adds that the Law, as well, doesn't bring righteousness; instead, it brings wrath because we can't keep it perfectly—and perfection is what it demands. But if there were no law, then there would be no rules or stipulations to break.

Faith Is Bound to Grace

With works, ritual, and the Law all coming up short, Paul concludes that the only way to a right standing with God is faith in His magnanimous grace.

> For this reason it is by faith, in order that it may be in accordance with grace, so that the promise will be guaranteed to all the descendants, not only to those who are of the Law, but also to those who are of the faith of Abraham, who is the father of us all (as it is written, "A father of many nations have I made you") in the presence of Him whom he believed. (vv. 16–17a)

Whether Jew ("those who are of the Law") or Gentile (those of the non-Law "faith of Abraham"), we come to God only through faith in His gracious provision of Jesus Christ. And because we are depending on God and not our own works—where we would never know if we'd done "enough"—we can rest in the assurance that we are saved, eternally secure, because we know that God keeps His word. Now we are living illustrations of His grace, just as Abraham was, who "is the father of us all."

Abraham's Hope

God had promised Abraham that he would be "a father of many nations" before the child of the promise was even born, remember? Abraham was ninety-nine years old when God uttered these words (see Gen. 17:1–5). Yet Abraham believed God, placing his faith in the One who gives life to the dead and calls into being that which does not exist. (Rom. 4:17b)

What a beautiful expression of God's power as the Creator and Resurrecter! With this knowledge of God as his focus, is it any wonder that Abraham, "in hope against hope,"

believed, so that he might become a father of many nations according to that which had been spoken, "So shall your descendants be." Without becoming weak in faith he contemplated his own body, now as good as dead since he was about a hundred years old, and the deadness of Sarah's womb; yet, with respect to the promise of God, he did not waver in unbelief but grew strong in faith, giving glory to God. (vv. 18–20)

Twenty-four years after God's initial promise to him, and despite the facts of his advanced age and Sarah's eighty-nine years of infertility, Abraham still clung to the reality of God's power and faithfulness. He believed that God would give life to the deadness of Sarah's womb and call into being a child and a nation which did not yet exist. In short, Abraham was

fully assured that what God had promised, He was able also to perform. (v. 21)

That kind of faith, the faith that endures over the long haul, gives glory to God. It trusts in God's truthfulness, and it hopes in His goodness. It is not blind faith, however.

Abraham "contemplated" or realized that he and Sarah were well beyond the child-bearing years, and he laughed and wondered about the impact of their own human limitations on God's promise (see Gen. 17:17). But he did not turn *away* from God in unbelief; rather, he turned *to* Him with his concerns and believed the answer God gave him (17:18–27). His growing and deepening faith in God honored the Lord, or as John Stott puts it,

He glorified God by letting God be God, and by trusting him to be true to himself as the God of creation and resurrection.[3]

---

3. John Stott, *Romans: God's Good News for the World* (Downers Grove, Ill.: InterVarsity Press, 1994), p. 134.

This faith, which was anchored in God's character, was credited to Abraham as righteousness (Rom. 4:22). And this faith was rewarded a year later with a little son, Isaac, whose name, "he laughs," reflects the joy of God's incredible grace.

Abraham's Faith and Us

Now, Paul has not taken the Roman readers and us back to Abraham's story just for a "blast from the past." He has indeed given us a history lesson—but it's a history that we're a part of, a history that is still going on.

> The words "it was credited to him" were written not for him alone, but also for us, to whom God will credit righteousness—for us who believe in him who raised Jesus our Lord from the dead. He was delivered over to death for our sins and was raised to life for our justification. (vv. 23–25 NIV)

Like Abraham, when we believe in the One who "gives life to the dead"—as God raised Jesus from the dead and as He raises us from spiritual deadness—and the One who "calls into being that which did not exist"—a holy kingdom made of justified sinners like us—then we have put our faith in the right place. Not in works, not in ceremonies and rituals, not in rule keeping. But in the all-powerful and always faithful God, through His Son, Jesus Christ, who has redeemed us with His own blood and raises us to new life by His resurrection. And who reaches out to us, looks after us, and promises us blessings beyond our wildest dreams because of His unending love.

✝ *Living Insights*

After studying a passage like Romans 4, it would be easy to start wishing we had a faith like Abraham's, wouldn't it? A stalwart faith that *never* wavers, a strong faith that *never* doubts, a stoic faith that *never* falters.

Wait a minute! Abraham didn't have a faith as perfect as that. No human being can have a faith as perfect as that, because no human being is perfect. To set ourselves up with such an unrealistic standard is to set ourselves up for despair. And that's not what Paul wanted to do at all.

He wanted to show that faith is the only way we can be saved and justified by God. And his focus was not on the quality and quantity of our faith, but on *the One in whom our faith is placed.* Faith isn't something to take pride in like a human work or merit; rather, it produces humility and gratitude. It shouldn't put the faithful one's name in lights but instead should be a searchlight drawing attention to God and His grace. Having faith is not about how much faith we can muster but about how much we know and can count on the Lord.

Take some time to search through the Scriptures and reflect on God's character. Start out with the references listed below, then feel free to add more as you explore any cross-references listed in your Bible's marginal notes.

Deuteronomy 10:18 _____

_____

2 Chronicles 16:9 _____

_____

Nehemiah 9:17b _____

_____

Psalm 34:8 _____

_____

Psalm 89:14 _____

_____

Psalm 90:2 _____

_____

Psalm 136 _____

_____

Isaiah 6:3 _____

Isaiah 30:18 _____

Jeremiah 9:24 _____

Matthew 11:29 _____

Romans 4:17b _____

Romans 4:21 _____

Romans 15:5 _____

Romans 15:13 _____

1 Corinthians 14:33 _____

2 Corinthians 1:3 _____

Ephesians 2:4 _____

2 Timothy 2:13 _____

Hebrews 11:6 _____

_____

1 John 1:5 _____

_____

1 John 3:1; 4:8 _____

_____

1 John 3:5 _____

_____

1 John 3:8b _____

_____

Other references _____

_____

_____

_____

_____

_____

_____

_____

As Christians, we nourish our faith by deepening our understanding of the Object of our faith. May Peter's benediction be our life's aim, now and always:

> Grow in the grace and knowledge of our Lord and Savior Jesus Christ. To Him be the glory, both now and to the day of eternity. Amen. (2 Pet. 3:18)

Chapter 11
UNQUENCHABLE OPTIMISM
Romans 5:1–11

It ain't braggin' if you can back it up."

Have you ever heard this saying? Maybe you heard it from your Uncle Earl when you were a kid. You remember Uncle Earl. He seemed to be an expert at everything from backyard badminton to wrastlin' to catchin' catfish. And, in addition to being an expert in stuff all-important to ten-year-olds, he always had something to say about his impending performance.

"Watch me sink the four-ball in the corner pocket."

"I bet I hook a trout in the next five minutes."

"I'll spot you fourteen points and beat you 15–14."

Of course, Uncle Earl was never officially "bragging" because he regularly backed up his words with his actions. He consistently made good on his boasts.

Christians, too, have a right to boast—not in ourselves, but in Christ. We can proclaim with certainty that we will be spending eternity in heaven because of the certainty of Christ's character and work.

Unfortunately, though many of us believe this in our hearts, we somehow can't get it out of our mouths. We hesitate to make known our hopes of a bright future because of doubt's nagging whisper: *What if we're wrong?*

In Romans 5:1–11, Paul assures us that our hope in God will never disappoint us. Heaven is not wishful thinking—it's a certainty. What an unquenchable optimism this can give us! Our future glory is not empty bragging, because it's backed up by a God who always keeps His promises.

The Positional Benefits of Justification

Paul ended Romans 4 on an important note: "He who was delivered over because of our transgressions, and was raised because of our *justification*" (v. 25, emphasis added). Heaven comes as a result of our justification, but we can enjoy many of God's rich blessings even before we get to heaven.

The benefits we receive from being justified can be organized into two categories. First, we experience "positional" benefits that describe our new standing before God in His court. We no longer appear before Him as condemned sinners. Rather, our crimes have been paid for by our Savior, and because we've accepted that payment through faith, we enjoy our new status as justified believers (see 3:21–24). These positional benefits are objective truths; they never change. Neither our feelings nor our opinions can alter them. Let's take a look at the benefits Paul enumerates in Romans 5:1–2a.

We Have Peace with God

The first benefit we enjoy is peace with God.

> Therefore, having been justified by faith, we have
> peace with God through our Lord Jesus Christ. (v. 1)

Did you know that before we were justified through faith in Christ, we were at war with God? Colossians 1:21 describes us as having been "alienated and hostile" toward Him. And Romans 5:10 says we were former "enemies" of God. Imagine that—being in a state of militant hostility toward the Ruler of the universe, and worse, having Him in a state of enmity toward us. What a mismatch! Fortunately, our faith in Jesus Christ has saved us from becoming a casualty in this conflict.

Through faith, we raised the white flag of surrender and became whiter than snow. We dropped to our knees in defeat and gained spiritual victory. With one stroke of faith, we signed a peace treaty with the Almighty and enlisted in His holy army of redeemed sinners. We are now at peace with God.

The term *peace*, however, means more than a simple cease-fire of animosities. It also connotes a relationship of well-being, prosperity, and good intentions. In this sense, it parallels the Hebrew word *shalom*.[1] So, not only do we experience a lack of hostility toward and from God, we also enter into a joyfully loving relationship with Him.

Didn't we say, though, that positional benefits, such as peace, are objective truths that don't depend on feelings? Yes, but objective truths can naturally produce emotions within us. The assurance of

---

1. See Douglas Moo, *Romans 1–8*, The Wycliffe Exegetical Commentary series, gen. ed. Kenneth Barker (Chicago, Ill.: Moody Press, 1991), p. 306.

peace gives us a sense of relief and tranquility. As John Witmer notes, "A believer is not responsible for having peace in the sense of making it but in the sense of enjoying it."[2] That's one responsibility few people would find hard to bear!

We Stand in Grace

In addition to having peace with God, we also stand in His grace.

> Through whom also we have obtained our introduction by faith into this grace in which we stand. (Rom. 5:2a)

The term *introduction* describes a formal meeting in which a common person would be ushered into the presence of royalty or some other person of high station. Our faith, then, has introduced us into our King's presence, and we now stand in the realm of His grace. We have been given the opportunity to live according to a new way of life. We are no longer required to adhere to the standards of the Law for God's acceptance. We are written into His will—heirs to a family fortune beyond our wildest imaginations. This positional benefit we have received—this entrance into the sphere of the Lord's grace—is due only to our justification by faith.

The Experiential Benefits of Justification

The second category of benefits we receive from our justification can be described as "experiential." Where the positional benefits are objective and independent of emotion, these experiential benefits are subjective and full of feeling. They describe the effects that the positional benefits have on us, and they deal with one emotion in particular—joy.

We Rejoice in Hope

Since joy is so closely linked to hope, let's jump ahead in the passage to see what Paul has to say about the primacy of hope.

> We exult in hope of the glory of God . . . having

---

2. John A. Witmer, "Romans," *The Bible Knowledge Commentary*, New Testament edition, ed. John F. Walvoord and Roy B. Zuck (Wheaton, Ill.: Scripture Press Publications, Victor Books, 1983), p. 456.

been justified by His blood, we shall be saved from the wrath of God through Him. For if while we were enemies we were reconciled to God through the death of His Son, much more, having been reconciled, we shall be saved by His life. (vv. 2b, 9b–10)

Our first expression of joy comes when we realize the hope we have in the future. Paul uses the Greek word *kauchaomai* for *exult*, which means literally "to boast" or "to take confidence in."[3] In other words, the term describes a kind of "bragging" in which we make bold statements based on our confidence in their fulfillment. This kind of hope differs from how most of us usually define the word.

We often take "hope" to mean wishful thinking. But that definition leaves hope's fulfillment completely open-ended. Paul, on the other hand, held a much different view. He used the term *hope* to communicate a confidence that his desires were foregone conclusions.[4] In Paul's mind, his salvation had already been fulfilled; only time was standing between him and his future glorification.

Glorification, then, is the object of our hope—it's what we hope for. Paul describes it as "the glory of God" (v. 2b), which is a phrase rich in meaning. It points to:

1. Our seeing Jesus when He returns in His full divine splendor,

2. Our transformation into His likeness—sinless and immortal, and

3. The renewal of creation to its perfect design.[5]

What a beautiful future we have to look forward to! So let's hope as Paul did—fully expecting our desires to become reality. Only then will we rejoice in our future the way God intended us to.

---

3. Moo, *Romans 1–8*, p. 309.

4. See Gerhard Kittel, ed. *Theological Dictionary of the New Testament*, trans. and ed. Geoffrey W. Bromiley (1964; reprint, Grand Rapids, Mich.: William B. Eerdmans Publishing Co., 1993), vol. 2, pp. 530, 532.

5. See John Stott, *Romans: God's Good News for the World* (Downers Grove, Ill.: InterVarsity Press, 1994), pp. 140–41.

We Rejoice in Suffering

After establishing the first type of joy, Paul sets off the other three with a parallel phrase:

> And not only this, but we also exult in our tribulations, knowing that tribulation brings about perseverance; and perseverance, proven character; and proven character, hope. (vv. 3–4)

Rejoice in tribulation? That doesn't seem to make much sense. Rejoicing in hope is logical—hope is a positive force; it makes us feel good. But joy and tribulation seem like oil and water—they just don't mix. Even worse, they often react like fire on tinder: the heat of oppression often burns away any joy we might have. So why would Paul make trials a source of joy for the Christian?

Because we harvest a rich crop of spiritual maturity when God sows tribulation into our lives. When we endure suffering in faith, we learn perseverance. Persevering, in turn, produces proven character —character that has passed the test, so to speak. Then character brings forth hope, "perhaps because the God who is developing our character in the present can be relied on for the future too."[6]

What Christian doesn't want to exemplify these qualities? Yet they come only through trusting Christ during tribulation. Because of this, believers can take joy in suffering, knowing that God is watering their faith and causing them to grow in Him.

Look at what Paul says next.

> And hope does not disappoint, because the love of God has been poured out within our hearts through the Holy Spirit who was given to us. (v. 5)

We're back to hope again. In the middle of tribulation, our hope in God is not an empty hope. We can be assured of our certain future, even in the midst of hardship, because it is in hardship that God delights to display His love.

The *and* at the beginning of this verse connects the thought to the previous one, showing us that God's love somehow relates to our suffering. But how does it relate? We know from other passages in Scripture that God's love sustains us through suffering, and this truth certainly serves as a source of hope for us.

---

6. Stott, *Romans: God's Good News for the World*, p. 142

But the structure of Romans 5:3–5 seems to indicate that God uses our tribulations as opportunities to remind us of His love for us. How does He remind us? By pouring His love into our hearts through the Holy Spirit, whom He has given to us as a gift. The Spirit, then, makes us "deeply and refreshingly aware that God loves us."[7]

How do we know He loves us? As Paul next tells us, Christ is the portrait and the proof of His love.

> For while we were still helpless, at the right time
> Christ died for the ungodly. For one will hardly die
> for a righteous man; though perhaps for the good
> man someone would dare even to die. But God dem-
> onstrates His own love toward us, in that while we
> were yet sinners, Christ died for us. (vv. 6–8)

The gift Christ gave us on the cross proves God's love beyond any shadow of a doubt. And not only did it confirm the reality of God's love, it also demonstrated the degree of that love.

When a gift is given, the degree of love behind the gift can be measured in two ways—partly by the costliness of the gift to the giver, and partly by the worthiness of the one receiving the gift. When Christ died on the cross, the cost to God could not have been higher, and we could not have been less worthy of His love. Therefore, we can rejoice because we know God loves us—loves us even to the point of sacrificing His own Son on our behalf.

We Rejoice in God

Finally, Paul introduces us to another type of joy we can expect to experience. Once again, he writes:

> And not only this, but we also exult in God through
> our Lord Jesus Christ, through whom we have now
> received the reconciliation. (v. 11)

What does it mean to exult—to boast—in God? To answer this question, we need to turn back to Romans 2:17–29. There Paul denounced the Jews for boasting in God—for seeing them-selves as morally superior to others because God had given them the Law. He chastised them for their hypocrisy, which actually turned Gentiles away from God rather than drawing them to Him.

---

7. Stott, *Romans: God's Good News for the World*, p. 143.

After proving the Jews' guilt (chap. 2) and the guilt of the rest of the world (chap. 3), Paul made his case for justification by faith alone (chap. 4). But not until 5:11 does Paul return to the subject of boasting in God, and in this verse, he reveals what true boasting in the Lord entails. John Stott beautifully describes Paul's meaning.

> Christian exultation in God begins with the shame-faced recognition that we have no claim on him at all, continues with wondering worship that while we were still sinners and enemies Christ died for us, and ends with the humble confidence that he will complete the work he has begun. So to exult in God is to rejoice not in our privileges but in his mercies, not in our possession of him but in his of us.[8]

The final benefit we receive from our justification, then, is a joy that comes only from the humble recognition that, while we were completely undeserving, God reconciled us to Himself through His Son.

☩ *Living Insights*

Wouldn't it be great to live in God's peace, grace, hope, and joy during your daily routine? It may be more likely than you think. A lot of it has to do with your mind-set. In light of this, take a few minutes to think through the following questions.

What have you been focusing on lately? Your problems, limitations, past mistakes? Your ambitions, maybe, like acquiring material goods, achieving a certain status, or gaining others' approval? How often do you contemplate the peace you have with God because of Christ? His grace to you? Your eternal destiny with Him?

---

8. Stott, *Romans: God's Good News for the World*, pp. 147–48.

How can knowing what God has already done for you help you through what you face today?

_____

_____

_____

_____

_____

What we focus on plays a large part in determining our attitude. How would you describe the state of your attitude most of the time? Worried? Defeated? Fearful? Hopeful? Grateful? Optimistic? How has your focus impacted your attitude?

_____

_____

_____

_____

_____

What does your attitude communicate to others about God?

_____

_____

_____

_____

What would you like your life to say about God? Prayerfully consider how you can begin to accomplish this.

_____

_____

_____

_____

From what you have discovered, what do you need to do to keep joy alive in your Christian experience?

_____

_____

_____

_____

_____

_____

_____

_____

_____

_____

_____

_____

_____

_____

_____

_____

Chapter 12

MAN OF GUILT ...
MAN OF GRACE

Romans 5:12–21

I t was the best of times, it was the worst of times."

This is how Charles Dickens began his epic A *Tale of Two Cities*, which chronicles not only the history of two cities but the lives of two men whose paths crossed during the French Revolution.

In Romans 5, the apostle Paul also tells a tale of two men: Adam, a man of guilt, and Jesus, a man of grace. If Dickens were to paraphrase Paul, he might say that Adam represents the worst of times and Jesus, the best. Or he might tell the story as follows.

A long time ago, in a land far, far away, a glorious King ruled a land called Eden. Two of the King's servants—a man and his wife—lived together in a beautiful garden and tended it for the King. In His great kindness, the King provided for their every need.

In the cool of the evening, the King would join the man and woman, and they would walk the grounds and enjoy all that the sanctuary had to offer—cool grass under bare feet, sumptuous fruits of every kind, flowers of every hue, warm sunlight, and gentle breezes. There was perfect harmony between King and servants . . . for awhile.

The King allowed the man and the woman to enjoy every part of the garden—except one. The fruit from one tree that stood in the middle of the garden was forbidden. One day, however, an enemy of the King who lived outside Eden sneaked inside the garden and waited in the shadow of the tree for the man and the woman to pass by. When they did, he whispered from the dark and enticed the woman to eat of the

87

tree's fruit. She ate and gave some to her husband.

Because of their insurrection, harmony between the King and His servants disintegrated, and the King banished them from His perfect kingdom. The man and the woman, and all their descendants, were now destined to suffer the King's judgment for their betrayal—and that judgment was a death sentence. But the loving King already had a plan to rescue them from their spiritual exile.

The King sent His Son to deliver the man and woman and their children from the sentence of death. To do this, the Son had to die in their place and reconcile them to the King. Out of love, the Son willingly offered Himself up for execution. He died, paying the penalty required by the King's law and enabling the descendants of the man and woman to return to the King.

❦

The final chapter of A *Tale of Two Cities* contains the words, "It is a far, far better thing that I do, than I have ever done," spoken by the hero who died for his friend. And the same is true of Jesus Christ. It is a far better thing that He has done—laid down His life for sinners—than anyone has ever done . . . or ever will do. And His words can still be heard today: "I am the resurrection and the life; he who believes in Me will live even if he dies, and everyone who lives and believes in Me will never die."

Christ alone has paid the price for humanity's sin. Out of love, He performed an act of grace that leads to eternal life for all those who trust Him. He alone came to undo Adam's act of rebellion that leads to death.

The apostle Paul's inspired version of the story in Romans 5:12–21 reminds us that a very clear choice lies before us: the way of the man of guilt or the way of the Man of grace. Which do you choose?

Adam: The Cause of Our Guilt

Paul begins this second half of Romans 5 by explaining the effects of the rebellion committed by the first man, Adam. Through him, Paul reveals, sin and death entered the human race and spread to all people. And the Law, contrary to what many think, mainly functioned to magnify these two destructive forces.

The Entrance of Sin and Death

In verse 12, Paul shows that the idea of one man affecting the many, as Christ does for our good (vv. 9–11), is not a new idea at all. It has been a fact since the beginning of the human race.

> Therefore, just as through one man sin entered into
> the world, and death through sin . . .[1] (Rom. 5:12a)

Sin entered the world through "one man." Paul doesn't name Adam here, but he's obviously the one the apostle had in mind. In particular, Paul was referring to the events recorded in Genesis 3:6.

> When the woman saw that the tree was good for food, and that it was a delight to the eyes, and that the tree was desirable to make one wise, she took from its fruit and ate; and she gave also to her husband with her, and he ate.

This tree was the one God had forbidden Adam to eat from (2:16–17). By eating its fruit, Adam disobeyed God, thus contaminating human existence with sin. With sin came death—the natural consequence of sin that God had warned him about (v. 17).

The word "death" has several meanings in this passage. First, it refers to immediate spiritual death and eventual physical death. Second, it refers to separation—both the physical separation of being removed from the garden of Eden and the spiritual separation of losing intimacy with God.

The Spread of Both to All

Sin and death spread far beyond just Adam and Eve. As history and the Scriptures show us, these destructive forces spread to all humanity.

> And so death spread to all men, because all sinned. (Rom. 5:12b)

---

1. Paul starts a train of thought in verse 12 that he really doesn't complete, it seems, until verse 18. His whole thought may have read something like this: "Just as through one man sin entered into the world, and death through sin, so through one act of righteousness there resulted justification of life to all men."

What did Paul mean when he wrote "all sinned"? We weren't present when Adam took a bite out of the fruit, so how can we be held responsible for a sin we didn't commit? Theologians tell us that Adam was acting as our "federal head"—the representative of the whole human race. Therefore, any action he took, he took on behalf of the whole species. As a result, when he sinned, "all sinned." And when he was sentenced to death, so were we. Universal sin led to universal death,[2] making us, too, physically and spiritually separated from God.

Sin and the Law

"But," a Jew in Paul's audience might have retorted, "there can be no sin apart from the Law. And the Law did not exist when Adam sinned. Therefore, there can be no sin on Adam's part, and because there can be no sin, there can be no death!"

To this clever yet flawed insight, Paul responds:

> For until the Law sin was in the world, but sin is not imputed when there is no law. Nevertheless death reigned from Adam until Moses, even over those who had not sinned in the likeness of the offense of Adam, who is a type of Him who was to come. (vv. 13–14)

Paul makes it clear "that even without the law to define sin sharply (13b), both sin (13a) and death (14) were present and powerful."[3]

In the midst of these dismal circumstances that the man of guilt got us into, Paul now turns to the Man of grace.

Christ and Adam: Contrast and Comparison

As Christ, the second Adam, enters the scene, Paul shows both the differences and the similarities between Him and the first Adam.

Contrast

Paul begins by noting three ways in which Jesus differs from Adam: (1) in the nature of His actions, (2) in the spiritual consequences

2. See John Stott, *Romans: God's Good News for the World* (Downers Grove, Ill.: InterVarsity Press, 1994), p. 150.

3. Douglas Moo, *Romans 1–8*, The Wycliffe Exegetical Commentary series, gen. ed. Kenneth Barker (Chicago, Ill.: Moody Press, 1991), p. 341.

of His actions, and (3) in the experiential results of His actions. Let's contrast the nature of Jesus' and Adam's actions first.

> But the free gift is not like the transgression. For if by the transgression of the one the many died, much more did the grace of God and the gift by the grace of the one Man, Jesus Christ, abound to the many. (v. 15)

Did you catch the difference between the kind of action each man took? Adam's action, disobeying God's explicit command by eating the fruit, was a "transgression"—an act of rebellion. Christ's action, on the other hand, was a gift—a gesture of grace and reconciliation in which He died in our place. The two men's actions were completely different in their nature, one man sinning in self-asserting pride and the other giving a gift of selfless sacrifice.

In addition to this contrast in nature, Paul also points out a difference in the spiritual consequences of their actions.

> The gift is not like that which came through the one who sinned; for on the one hand the judgment arose from one transgression resulting in condemnation, but on the other hand the free gift arose from many transgressions resulting in justification. (v. 16)

Whereas Adam's sin led to condemnation, Christ's sacrifice led to justification. Because of Adam's sin, all people stand before God as guilty sinners. By trusting in Christ, people receive forgiveness and a new standing before God.

Finally, Paul contrasts the experiential results brought on by each man's actions.

> For if by the transgression of the one, death reigned through the one, much more those who receive the abundance of grace and of the gift of righteousness will reign in life through the One, Jesus Christ. (v. 17)

Adam's sin resulted in death; Christ's gift results in life. But these two forces—death and life—do more than simply exist. They reign—like a king on a throne. And all people live under the rulership of one of these kings. Either they live under the dominion of death or they reside in the kingdom of life. Only those who have trusted in Christ have life.

Comparison

Paul now moves from describing the differences between Adam and Christ to showing a point of similarity between the two.

> So then as through one transgression there resulted condemnation to all men, even so through one act of righteousness there resulted justification of life to all men. For as through the one man's disobedience the many were made sinners, even so through the obedience of the One the many will be made righteous. (vv. 18–19)

Did you notice the point of similarity? Both men acted as representatives of the human race. Adam stepped forward and sinned against God, incurring His judgment on us all. Christ, however, stood in our place, taking our guilt upon Himself and appeasing God's wrath so that we could receive forgiveness. As John Stott puts it, "The one act of the one man determined the destiny of the many"[4]—one for bad, one for good.

We can sum up the contributions of Adam and Christ in the following chart.

| The Contributions of Adam and Christ ||
Adam	Christ
Transgression	Gift of grace
Condemnation	Justification
Death	Life
Disobedience	Obedience
Many made sinners	Many made righteous
Sin reigned in death	Grace reigns in righteousness, bringing life

Christ: The Source of Our Grace

In the third and final section of Romans 5:12–21, Paul turns his focus to Christ alone. In particular, he emphasizes the gift Christ has given us—grace. In regard to this grace, the text reveals two prominent features.

---

4. Stott, *Romans*, p. 156.

Grace Abounds

First, Christ's gift of grace is extremely abundant.

> The Law came in so that the transgression would
> increase; but where sin increased, grace abounded
> all the more. (v. 20)

The Law came to point people to the central figure of God's
plan of redemption—Jesus. The Law accomplishes this mission by
"intensifying" sin—by showing people the ways in which they have
transgressed against God. Without the Law, humanity may never
have known the extent of its guilt. By formalizing God's standard
into a code, the Law makes our sinfulness explicit to us.[5]

Though sin increased, however, God's grace increased all the
more. No matter how guilty we are, no matter how many of God's
laws we've broken, the grace of Christ reaches further. The phrase
"abounded all the more" is actually a single, compound word in the
Greek, *superabounds*, and is used only one other time in the Bible
(see 2 Cor. 7:4). This word clearly shows that Christ's forgiveness
and grace always exceed the amount of our sin.[6]

Grace Reigns

Second, the grace of Christ reigns.

> So that, as sin reigned in death, even so grace would
> reign through righteousness to eternal life through
> Jesus Christ our Lord. (v. 21)

This is God's goal—that grace would reign through righteousness in order to bring eternal life to all who trust in Christ.[7] What
idea could better sum up Romans 1–5 than the idea of the rulership
of grace? John Stott notes:

> For grace forgives sins through the cross, and bestows
> on the sinner both righteousness and eternal life.

---

5. See *The Nelson Study Bible*, gen. ed. Earl D. Radmacher (Nashville, Tenn.: Thomas Nelson
Publishers, 1997), p. 1888.

6. See Robert H. Mounce, *The New American Commentary: Romans* (Nashville, Tenn.:
Broadman and Holman Publishers, 1995), vol. 27, p. 145.

7. See John A. Witmer, "Romans," in *The Bible Knowledge Commentary*, New Testament
edition, ed. John F. Walvoord and Roy B. Zuck (Wheaton, Ill.: Scripture Press Publications,
Victor Books, 1983), p. 461.

Grace satisfies the thirsty soul and fills the hungry with good things. Grace sanctifies sinners, shaping them into the image of Christ. Grace perseveres even with the recalcitrant, determining to complete what it has begun. And one day grace will destroy death and consummate the kingdom. So when we are convinced that "grace reigns," we will remember that God's throne is a "throne of grace", and will come to it boldly to receive mercy and to find grace for every need.[8]

And just as Paul began by focusing on the first man Adam, he closes by uplifting the other, better Man—Jesus Christ our Lord.

✝ Living Insights

I hope you don't think that's all there is to this tale of two men. Because *you're* part of the story. You live every day touched by the reality of how Adam and Christ lived . . . and died. So take some time to let the truth of Romans 5:12–21 seep into your present circumstances by answering the following questions.

Reread John Stott's quote about grace at the end of the lesson. What does it tell you about God's complete commitment to your spiritual growth . . . even when you fail?

_____

_____

_____

_____

_____

_____

_____

_____

8. Stott, *Romans*, pp. 157–58.

Consider for a moment any difficulties, disappointments, worries, insecurities, and conflicts you're facing right now. What hope do Stott's (and Paul's) words give you for continuing in the Christian life?

_____

_____

_____

_____

_____

The Christian life is the only real "happily ever after" story, because our Lord is with us and will lead us through this life—with all its trials—to the next one—where there is only joy. All because of Christ and His grace. And that's no fairy tale, no fable. It is our destiny.

BOOKS FOR
PROBING FURTHER

How blessed we are to live in an age when so many expositional and theological works—produced throughout history—are available to enrich our understanding of Paul's letter to the Romans. If you want to dig deeper into some of the themes he explores, we recommend the following books for your study.

Barnhouse, Donald Grey. *Expositions of Bible Doctrines, Taking the Epistle to the Romans as a Point of Departure.* 4 vols. 1952–64. Reprint, Grand Rapids, Mich.: William B. Eerdmans Publishing Co., 1988.

Barton, Bruce B., David R. Veerman, Neil Wilson. *Romans.* Life Application Bible Commentary Series. Wheaton, Ill.: Tyndale House Publishers, 1992.

Boice, James Montgomery. *Romans, Volume 1: Justification by Faith (Romans 1–4).* Grand Rapids, Mich.: Baker Book House, 1991.

———. *Romans, Volume 2: The Reign of Grace (Romans 5:1–8:39).* Grand Rapids, Mich.: Baker Book House, 1992.

Bunyan, John. *The Pilgrim's Progress.* Reprint, Grand Rapids, Mich.: Baker Book House, 1984.

Calvin, John. *Institutes of the Christian Religion.* Translated by Ford Lewis Battles. Vols. 20 and 21 of *The Library of Christian Classics.* Ed. John T. McNeill. Philadelphia, Pa.: Westminster Press, 1960.

Luther, Martin. *The Bondage of the Will.* Translated by James I. Packer and O. R. Johnston. Grand Rapids, Mich.: Fleming H. Revell, 1957.

Morris, Leon. *The Epistle to the Romans.* 1988. Reprint, Grand Rapids, Mich.: William B. Eerdmans Publishing Co., 1992.

Packer, J. I. *Knowing God.* Downers Grove, Ill.: InterVarsity Press, 1973.

Plantinga, Cornelius, Jr.. *Not the Way It's Supposed to Be: A Breviary of Sin.* Grand Rapids, Mich.: William B. Eerdmans Publishing Co., 1995.

Sproul, R. C. *Faith Alone: The Evangelical Doctrine of Justification.* Grand Rapids, Mich.: Baker Books, 1995.

Stott, John. *Romans: God's Good News for the World.* Downers Grove, Ill.: InterVarsity Press, 1994.

Swindoll, Charles R. *Growing Deep in the Christian Life.* Portland, Ore.: Multnomah Press, 1986.

Walvoord, John F., and Roy B. Zuck, eds. *The Bible Knowledge Commentary.* New Testament edition. Wheaton, Ill.: Scripture Press Publications, Victor Books, 1983.

Some of the books listed may be out of print and available only through a library. For those currently available, please contact your local Christian bookstore. Books by Charles R. Swindoll may be obtained through Insight for Living, as well as some books by other authors.

Insight for Living also offers study guides on many books of the Bible, as well as on a variety of issues and Bible characters. For more information, see the ordering instructions that follow and contact the office that serves you.

Ordering Information

Coming to Terms with Sin

If you would like to order additional study guides, purchase the cassette series that accompanies this guide, or request our product catalogs, please contact the office that serves you.

United States and International locations:

Insight for Living
Post Office Box 69000
Anaheim, CA 92817-0900

1-800-772-8888, 24 hours a day, 7 days a week
(714) 575-5000, 8:00 A.M. to 4:30 P.M., Pacific time, Monday to Friday

Canada:

Insight for Living Ministries
Post Office Box 2510
Vancouver, BC, Canada V6B 3W7

1-800-663-7639, 24 hours a day, 7 days a week

Australia:

Insight for Living, Inc.
General Post Office Box 2823 EE
Melbourne, VIC 3001, Australia

(03) 9877-4277, 8:30 A.M. to 5:00 P.M., Monday to Friday

World Wide Web:

www.insight.org

Study Guide Subscription Program

Study guide subscriptions are available. Please call or write the office nearest you to find out how you can receive our study guides on a regular basis.